WORRY-FREE
RRSPs

Also by Richard Birch

THE FAMILY FINANCIAL PLANNING BOOK:
a step-by-step money guide for Canadian families

WORRY-FREE
RRSPs

Richard Birch

General
— PAPERBACKS —
Toronto, Canada

General Paperbacks edition
published in 1989

Published in 1988 by Stoddart Publishing Co. Limited

Published in 1987 by Methuen Publications

ISBN 0-7736-7225-7

Text Design: Brant Cowie/ArtPlus

Printed in U.S.A.

Disclaimer

The RRSP investing program outlined in this book is intended as a general guide only. The program may not be suitable for every individual. Recommendations for the purchase of specific investments are not provided, except in the case of Canada Savings Bonds. You, the reader, must make the final investment decision and choose the particular mutual fund investment for your RRSP. If you have any doubts or questions about your RRSP investing program, you are urged to consult with a tax, legal, investment or other financial counsellor. This book is sold on the understanding that the publisher and the author cannot be held responsible for any omissions or errors in the text, nor for the specific investment results you may obtain with your RRSPs.

Contents

Author's Note

Once again I offer my thanks to Gord Riehl, tax partner with Deloitte Haskins & Sells, for the support he has given me over the years. I am also grateful for the review, comments, and ideas provided by Pat Bouwers and Lucy Terk, tax managers with Deloitte Haskins & Sells, Sid Himmel, a chartered accountant, Stephen Yeung, account executive with Merrill Lynch Canada, and David Nunn, account executive with Wood Gundy. Any errors or omissions are, of course, my responsibility. I also want to thank Junia Fulgence for all her help.

My wife, Betsy Matthews, deserves the most thanks — for everything.

And yet another time, the proposals to change RRSPs have been delayed — this time by one year, to 1991. The technical details on RRSPs are based on legislation in effect as of May 1989 and on pension reform proposals released by the federal and several provincial governments up to May 1989, including the federal retirement savings draft legislation released on March 28, 1988, by Finance Minister Michael Wilson. These proposals, with the August revisions, are not expected to become law until 1990. You may want to confirm certain aspects of the current or proposed law with a tax professional or an official at your local district taxation office.

CHAPTER ONE

RRSPs
Your Key to a Secure Future

H OW IMPORTANT are RRSPs to the average Canadian? With recent advances in medicine and workers opting for earlier retirement, it is entirely possible that you will be retired for about the same number of years that you work. This means that for every 12 months that you are in the work force, you must earn enough to support yourself, and those depending on you, for 24 months — one year now and one year in the not-too-distant future.

You are going to need all the help you can muster! Fortunately, help is as close as around the corner where you do your banking, and it is spelled R-R-S-P, which stands for registered retirement savings plan.

A surprising number of Canadian workers — perhaps as many as three or four million — have *never* used an RRSP. Many think that RRSPs are only for the rich. Many others are confused by the barrage of RRSP advertising in January and February each year. The choices are so mind-boggling that many opt to ignore RRSPs rather than take a chance on making the wrong decision. And a great number of Canadians think that RRSPs are just too complicated to bother with.

The truth is that RRSPs don't have to be complex or confusing. That's why I wrote this book — to convince you that RRSPs can be used successfully by *all* workers, both employed and self-employed, and to show you how to easily thread your way through the RRSP jungle. For the average Canadian, RRSPs are *almost* as easy to deal with as your bank account. Okay, they are a bit more complicated, but you have a lot more at stake with an

1

RRSP — getting through 20 or 30 or maybe even 40 years of retirement.

Another three or four million Canadians *have* contributed to an RRSP at some point. However, a great number of these have adopted the *ostrich* approach. They write a cheque for the first RRSP that catches their eye, usually where they bank, provide some basic personal information, and try not to give the RRSP another thought. The next year their bank (or trust company, credit union, savings and loan corporation, or *caisse populaire*) notifies them that it is time to make another RRSP contribution. Instead of examining what they earned on last year's RRSP contribution and doing a bit of RRSP comparison shopping, they write another cheque. These workers will be further ahead than those who do not contribute, but they could be *a lot better off*.

The second objective of this book is to help you get your RRSP working more effectively for you. If you contribute a few dollars to your RRSP each year and earn only what savings accounts pay, perhaps four or five per cent, you are not going to accumulate very much for your retirement years. And it may feel like a lot less if inflation averages four or five per cent. It's easy to do better — a lot better — and it takes very little effort to get there.

The third and final goal of this book is to show you how to get the most out of your RRSP when you do retire. This means having as much as possible saved in the RRSP, and, as a consequence, being able to arrange a retirement income that satisfies all your needs as long as you and your dependants live. Perhaps most important, it means arranging a retirement income that takes into account what inflation will do to your income during your retirement years.

Along the way, this book will explain the few RRSP rules that you should be aware of, including those that will help you avoid problems. It will also show you a few basic techniques that will help your RRSP grow more quickly, and it will answer the more common questions Canadians have about RRSPs and how RRSPs fit into their financial lives.

What Can an RRSP Do for You?

"I'm saving now and doing alright. Why bother with an RRSP? What more can it do for me?"

The answer is *lots more.*

What is an RRSP? They were mentioned earlier in the same breath with a savings account. They are similar in many respects. With the most common type of RRSP, you buy an RRSP-qualified investment (usually referred to as contributing to your RRSP). The process is no more complicated or time-consuming than opening a bank account and depositing a sum of money. In fact, a daily interest savings account qualifies as an RRSP investment.

However, an RRSP has two advantages that practically no other investment has, including bank accounts. First, you can contribute to an RRSP with pre-tax dollars. This simply means that if you earn $1,000 and contribute the entire amount to an RRSP, the Government *will not* levy any tax on that $1,000. (Actually, you deduct the amount contributed from income in your tax return, and your tax bill is reduced accordingly.) If you do not contribute to the RRSP, the Government will tax that $1,000, let's say at 40 per cent, leaving you with only $600. This is the amount that you will be able to deposit to the bank account. (With tax reform, a portion of your income will be taxed at about 40 per cent depending on which province you live in, if you earn from about $30,000 to $55,000 a year — it's unfortunately a fact that millions of average Canadians are in this 40 per cent tax bracket.)

The second advantage that RRSPs enjoy is that no tax is levied on the income earned inside the RRSP. Tax is payable only when you eventually receive funds from the RRSP. Interest earned in the savings account, on the other hand, will be taxed each year.

So how much better off are you with the RRSP compared with the savings account after, say, 30 years if each earns five per cent compounded annually? Almost *twice as well off* if you use the RRSP. (Compounding simply means that interest is earned on your interest.)

Only $600 can be deposited to the savings account since tax of $400 must be paid. And remember that tax must be paid each year on the interest earned. Thus, for each $5 of interest earned, tax of $2 must be paid (40 per cent of $5), leaving you with only $3 or a three per cent return in the savings account. At the end of 30 years, you will have about $1,450 in the savings account, after paying tax each year.

With the RRSP, you can contribute $1,000 instead of only $600, and you get to earn the full five per cent each year since income earned in an RRSP is not taxable. At the end of 30 years, you will have about $4,300 in the RRSP. Remember that tax is payable on the entire $4,300, but even if you pay tax at 40 per cent, you will be left with almost $2,600. Compare this with the $1,450 accumulated in the savings account. *Where would you rather have your savings?*

If the cost of living (inflation) is going up by five per cent a year and your RRSP is earning five per cent, it is unlikely that you are on the road to a secure and comfortable retirement. The second objective of this book is to help you get much more out of your RRSP.

Instead of earning five per cent with the savings account, let's say you buy a GIC type of RRSP (guaranteed investment certificate) that earns eight per cent compounded annually. At the end of 30 years, the RRSP will have grown to over $10,000, or after paying taxes at 40 per cent, to over $6,000. Thus, you have more than doubled the amount available for your retirement years.

However, you can still do better — probably a lot better. Let's say that after reading this book, you decide to contribute $1,200 to the RRSP instead of $1,000. You also arrange your RRSP investments so that you earn 15 per cent a year compounded annually, instead of eight per cent. And, you contribute the $1,200 to a spousal RRSP, which is explained in Chapter 5, so that tax is eventually paid at the rate of 25 per cent instead of 40 per cent. In this case, you will accumulate almost $80,000 in the RRSP. After paying taxes, you and your spouse will still have over $60,000 available.

That's $60,000 compared with the person who accumulates only $1,450 in the savings account. *Can you afford not to contribute to an RRSP, if at all possible?* And just think what will happen if you contribute every year for those 30 years?

There is no doubt that RRSPs will help you save, but what you really should be asking is: "What will RRSPs do for me when I'm retired?" Again the answer is *plenty*, perhaps everything — if you begin using them immediately.

For example, let's say that you earn $30,000 a year, and you can manage to contribute five per cent of your income, or $1,500 each year to your RRSP. To keep the example simple, we will assume that there is no inflation so that your income remains the same at $30,000 for 30 years. The RRSP earns nine per cent compounded annually (it would normally earn more if inflation were taken into account and your income would normally increase each year).

At the end of 30 years, you will have over $200,000 in your RRSP. In 1987, an annual retirement income for life of well over $20,000 could be arranged. If you combine this with Canada Pension Plan benefits, Old Age Security, and the fact that it costs less to live when you are retired (for example, you will no longer be making RRSP contributions), you should be as well off when you are retired as you are now. And if you contribute, say, eight or 10 per cent of your income to the RRSP each year (bearing in mind that there are limits on the amount that you may contribute), you could be much better off in your retirement years than you are now.

Unfortunately, only a minority of Canadians will achieve this kind of security. However, it is definitely within the reach of almost all Canadian workers.

The Step-by-Step Approach to RRSPs

There is no secret to getting the most out of your RRSP. And it can be done easily, with a minimum of time and energy. It is simply a matter of approaching your key to a secure future *step by step*. This book will show you how.

First, you determine how much you can contribute to your RRSP each year (a maximum limit is imposed). This is explained in Chapter 3. If you are married, both you and your partner should be contributing, if possible. Remember that you generally must be earning employment or self-employed income to be eligible to contribute to an RRSP.

Second, you invest your contributions according to the step-by-step formula outlined in Chapter 4. You need concern yourself with only three common, easy-to-understand investments. How much of each of the investments should be in your RRSP is determined by how many years away from retirement you are.

Third, you periodically monitor the progress of your RRSP investments — for many people, once a year is enough. As well, every so often you ensure that you are continuing to take advan-

tage of the basic techniques outlined in Chapters 2, 5, and 6 for
putting more muscle into the performance of your RRSP.

Finally, when you are within about a year of retiring, you
begin the process of converting your RRSP into a lifetime retirement income, which is explained in Chapter 7.

This step-by-step approach takes almost all of the time-consuming decision-making out of your involvement with RRSPs.
You don't have to worry about where to invest your contribution
each year — you know in advance exactly where your money is
going. You don't have to worry constantly about whether your
RRSP could be doing better or whether you own an investment
that is too risky — you will be investing for the long term and
relying on historical trends, rather than being whipsawed by day-
to-day fluctuations in the marketplace.

The watchword is *keep it simple!* Survey after survey has
demonstrated that average Canadians demand simplicity when
they are dealing with financial matters. They want their RRSPs to
be easy to deal with, to require little attention, and to provide
reasonable growth and good security.

No, RRSPs are not quite as simple to deal with as bank accounts. Then again, your RRSP will eventually do a lot more for
you than your bank account. A secure financial future for you
and your family is certainly worth a couple of hours each year.

CHAPTER TWO

Getting Started

A N RRSP is essentially a contract or agreement between you and a financial institution (the RRSP issuer or trustee) which exercises control over the plan. The agreement spells out a variety of things, most of which are highly technical and of little concern to the average Canadian. You will, however, be affected by one specific restriction: you are not permitted to receive funds directly from the RRSP unless you include them in income for tax purposes. In other words, you cannot make a contribution, get your tax refund, and then cancel the RRSP without a portion of the RRSP funds being paid back to the Government as tax. A number of other rules exist to prevent a few taxpayers from abusing the various RRSP privileges.

There are basically two types of RRSPs: depository and trusteed. The institution where you do your banking probably handles depository RRSPs. With these, you purchase an RRSP investment, perhaps a five-year GIC, and the bank registers the GIC as an RRSP. The amount that you paid for the GIC is deductible from income for tax purposes and your tax liability is reduced accordingly. The issuer sends you a receipt confirming the deductible amount. This receipt is included with your tax return.

Trusteed RRSPs are less common. With these, you generally provide the financial entity, perhaps a stockbroker, with cash, and the cash is used to make either a specific investment or perhaps a variety of investments. Self-directed (or self-administered) RRSPs come under this heading. Actually, the cash is deposited to the account of an *RRSP trust*, and the trust itself makes the investments. You can also transfer securities that you personally own to the RRSP trust and this counts as a contribution.

When you first begin making RRSP contributions, they will likely be the depository type. Later on, however, when you have built up a sizable amount in your RRSPs, you should consider switching to a trusteed self-directed RRSP. Your depository RRSPs can be easily switched over to a self-directed RRSP. Self-directed RRSPs are as simple or as complex as you want to make them. The one used in the step-by-step program outlined in Chapter 4 is in many ways easier to deal with than if you have several depository-type RRSPs.

As you may have gathered, you can have any number of RRSPs. Many people have only one and write a cheque to it each year. Others open up a different RRSP each year. This can lead to problems, especially if you have a dozen or more, which is not uncommon. A self-directed RRSP solves your problems since you can have a number of different investments under one roof and the issuer will keep track of them for you.

Where Can You Get an RRSP?

RRSPs are available from just about every financial institution in Canada, including: banks, trust companies, savings and loan corporations, credit unions, *caisses populaires* and insurance companies. As well, many investment funds (also called mutual funds) can be purchased as RRSPs, and stockbrokers also handle RRSPs. Investment fund RRSPs may be acquired through the fund itself, or you may have a broker or financial counsellor act as your agent for the purchase. Self-directed RRSPs are offered by many banks, trust companies and brokers.

To do the deed, you simply fill out the short agreement form or contract, sign it, and write a cheque. To contribute to this RRSP next year, it is as easy as putting a cheque in the mail. One trust company even lets you contribute by phone. Making your first RRSP contribution is covered in Chapter 4.

Now the Hard Part — Where Do You Get the Cash for Your Contribution?

Unfortunately, many Canadians simply do not have enough income to contribute to an RRSP. When over half of a person's wages is needed to pay the rent, this is not hard to understand.

Nevertheless, the great majority of Canadian workers do have enough to contribute every year. And those who are now contributing probably could manage quite a bit more.

The easiest way to ensure that you are contributing enough to an RRSP each and every year is to establish a regimented savings program that you stick to no matter what. Many people set aside a specific amount as soon as they receive their paycheques each month, and the funds are deposited immediately to their RRSP. This RRSP contribution is part of their monthly budget and is treated exactly the same as setting aside the grocery money. Many RRSP issuers have monthly contributory plans and will even arrange for automatic withdrawals from your bank account.

It can pay to look around for other sources of cash for your RRSP contribution. Many people have a surprisingly large amount of money in two or three or four different bank accounts. Of course, this cash is earning only four or five per cent interest annually. If you always have $500 or $1,000 extra in the bank, why not contribute it to an RRSP? As you will see later, it is almost as easy to get money out of an RRSP, should the need arise, as it is to get funds out of a savings account, although you will lose the tax benefits that you had gained with the RRSP.

Many Canadian workers buy Canada Savings Bonds (CSBs) on the payroll savings plan. Why not instead use the cash that is deducted from your paycheque as an RRSP contribution? For example, over a year it may cost you about $1,040 to buy a $1,000 CSB. The extra $40 is interest that you paid on money borrowed from the Government which was used to purchase the bond at the beginning of the year. There is every possibility that you will earn more with the RRSP than the rate of interest you were earning on the CSB.

For decades, insurance policies have been touted as a great way to save. As many of us discovered, they haven't been — and the insurance industry even recognizes this now. Many taxpayers have reorganized their life insurance and have managed to free up $300 or $400 and often more which they contribute to their RRSPs each year. They simply cancel their expensive policies, buy the cheapest term life insurance they can find to maintain their coverage, and deposit the difference in cost to the RRSP. If your life insurance savings were earning only four or five per cent a year (some older policies earn even less), it is not difficult to see how much further ahead you will eventually be with the RRSP, which could earn 10 or 15 per cent.

You probably do not have to look far to find other sources of cash to increase the size of your annual RRSP contribution. Many companies pay year-end bonuses. Why not put some or even all of this into your RRSP? Many Canadian families receive child tax credits. You can now receive a portion of your credits earlier in the year rather than waiting for a tax refund. Or how about putting every second family allowance cheque in your RRSP? Or the small inheritance you just received from Aunt Mabel? Or the few dollars you win on the lottery every so often? In fact, why not stop buying lottery tickets and contribute to your RRSP instead? The odds are overwhelmingly in favour of your RRSP providing much more cash for you and your family than the lottery ever will.

And most important, you should always contribute your tax refund to your RRSP. As noted in Chapter 1, you can contribute to RRSPs with pre-tax funds, whereas other investments must be made with after-tax funds. When you contribute to the RRSP you are able to deduct the amount from income and your taxes are reduced accordingly. Most employees who contribute to an RRSP end up receiving a tax refund in April or May.

It is best to contribute your anticipated tax refund immediately rather than waiting to actually receive it, if you have the cash available. For example, suppose that you are thinking of contributing $600 and your marginal tax rate is 40 per cent (your marginal tax rate is simply the highest rate of income tax that you pay). Instead, you should contribute $1,000 immediately, which generates a tax refund of $400 (40 per cent of $1,000). This leaves you in the same net position that you would otherwise be in if you were to always contribute your tax refunds — $600 of after-tax cash is contributed plus the $400 that is eventually paid back to you as a tax refund. This tactic allows your RRSP to grow much faster.

The concept of marginal income tax rates is extremely important to understand when making RRSP decisions. Under tax reform, there will be only three tax brackets. In 1989, the rates are as follows:

Federal Taxable Income	Tax Rate	Average Combined Federal and Provincial Rate
up to $27,802	17%	26%
$27,803 - $55,605	26%	40%
above $55,605	29%	45%

Your particular combined federal and provincial tax rate will vary depending on the province where you live, since each province taxes income at a different rate. Taxable income is income after taking certain deductions such as those for RRSP and pension plan contributions, union dues and child care expenses.

The following example explains how taxes at your marginal tax rate affect you. Assume that you earn $34,000. Since your total income is above $27,802 but less than $55,605, you are in the middle tax bracket. If you receive a $1,000 raise, you will pay tax at the rate of about 40 per cent, or $400, on that $1,000. This 40 per cent rate is your marginal rate of tax. Similarly, if you contribute that $1,000 to an RRSP, the tax saving you achieve will be at your 40 per cent marginal rate, or $400. In other words, if you do not make the RRSP contribution, you must pay tax of $400 on that particular $1,000 of income.

What Happens to Your Contributions?

An RRSP is nothing more than a way of investing. If you have a depository RRSP, you purchase an investment that is specially registered as an RRSP investment. If you contribute to a trusteed type of RRSP, the cash is used to purchase any type of investment as long as it qualifies under the RRSP rules. There are a huge variety of eligible RRSP investments ranging from savings accounts to exchange traded options. But if you want to get the most out of your RRSP and pay as little attention to it as possible, you only need to consider three:

• money market investment funds,
• equity investment funds, and
• Canada Savings Bonds.

The first two investments are mutual funds. You invest in the fund and the fund then invests your money. A money market fund invests primarily in short-term, government guaranteed interest-bearing securities, such as 30- or 90-day treasury bills. Many of these funds operate like a bank account, but pay a much higher rate of interest. Equity funds invest primarily in the blue chip shares of public companies listed on stock exchanges. The rate of return with equity funds has been extremely attractive over the long term, despite the October 1987 stock market crash. Most Canadians have purchased Canada Savings Bonds at one time or another. They are interest-bearing securities issued by the federal government which may be cashed at any time.

How to use these investments is explained in Chapter 4 and more detail on the investments is provided in Appendix A. Until you open a self-directed RRSP, you will generally be able to acquire only the first two investments with your RRSP cash.

Are RRSPs Safe?

How secure is your RRSP? — as secure as the issuing financial institution. Thus, you want to deal only with well-established entities that will be around for at least as long as you plan to be. However, there are other safeguards in place.

The most widely known is the $60,000 Canada Deposit Insurance Corporation plan (CDIC). All banks and many trust companies and savings and loan corporations are members. Under this plan, the total amount of your RRSPs that you have on deposit with a member is insured for up to $60,000 if the member institution gets into financial trouble. If you have RRSPs at several branches of the same entity, your coverage is limited to $60,000. But if you have RRSPs at several different institutions, all of which are CDIC members — for example at two different banks and three different trust companies — your coverage will total $300,000 (five times $60,000). The amounts you have on deposit outside your RRSP with CDIC members, such as a savings account, are separately insured for $60,000.

Credit unions, and *caisses populaires* in Quebec, also have an insurance system in place for the protection of deposits. And all stockbrokers are insured through their membership in the Investment Dealers' Association. Investment or mutual funds are not insured, but other safeguards exist. Deposits made with insurance companies are also not directly insured. However, most insurance company RRSPs have two advantages not found elsewhere: many guarantee to repay at least 75 per cent of the amount you invest if you cancel the RRSP, and almost all insurance company RRSPs are protected from creditors if you declare bankruptcy. Neither of these features is particularly important for most Canadian workers, although if you own your own business the creditor protection feature may be attractive.

Your best protection is to give your RRSP business only to those financial institutions that are at least a reasonable size, have been in business longer than most others, and have a profitable history. Don't begrudge the bank or trust company or credit union or broker a *reasonable* profit. If they are making money off your money, they will be around for a long time to come and should serve you well. A number of the investment funds have been in business for decades and currently manage over $1 billion in mutual fund and pension fund investments.

How Flexible Is Your RRSP?

An RRSP can be cancelled at any time. And some RRSPs permit the partial withdrawal of funds (this only took effect in 1986). It certainly happens occasionally that an RRSP has to be used to fund an emergency. And many people have used their RRSPs as the down payment on the purchase of their first home (see Chapter 6). Otherwise, you should try to leave your RRSP intact until you convert it into a retirement income. RRSPs are most beneficial when the earnings in the plan are allowed to compound over many years.

When you cancel an RRSP or withdraw funds from one, the amount must be included in your income for tax purposes. Since you had your taxes reduced when you made the RRSP contribution, it only makes sense that you must repay the taxes when you personally receive the RRSP funds. You will not receive the full amount that you requested from the issuer of your RRSP. Tax is withheld by the issuer and remitted to the Government, just as an employer withholds taxes from an employee's wages. You will get credit for the tax that is withheld when you file your income tax return.

Most RRSP issuers require that you notify them in advance if you plan to cancel an RRSP or withdraw funds from one. In many cases, it could take over a month to receive the funds. If your RRSP is a guaranteed investment, such as a GIC, you may not be able to cancel it until the GIC matures, which means that you might have to wait up to five years to cancel the RRSP. Other issuers will allow you to cancel GIC-type RRSPs but will, for instance, only pay you a savings account rate of interest on the amount invested, rather than the GIC interest rate.

If you do plan to take a sizable amount out of your RRSP, try to do it over two years. This should reduce the amount of tax you pay. As you well know, the higher your income is in a year, the higher the rate of tax levied on each additional dollar that is taxable. For example, if you withdraw $10,000 from an RRSP in one year, $5,000 may be taxed at 26 per cent and the other $5,000 at 40 per cent. However, if you receive $5,000 in December of this year and $5,000 a few days later in January, you might have more in your pocket since the whole $10,000 may be taxed at 26 per cent. Taxes may be reduced because the second $5,000 is included in your taxable income next year when it also might be taxed at 26 per cent.

Borrowing From Your RRSP

You are not permitted to borrow funds from your RRSP. If you somehow manage to do this, substantial penalties will apply. You also will be severely penalized if you use your RRSP as collateral or security for a loan.

However, there is one situation where you may borrow from your RRSP, namely, your RRSP can loan you funds in the form of a mortgage on your home. While it may appear attractive to pay your mortgage principal and interest to your own RRSP (of course, you must already have the cash in your RRSP), this is not recommended as an RRSP investment. Such an arrangement is suitable for only a few upper-income people, and you can generally do better over the long term with other investments.

Transfers Between RRSPs

If you are not happy with the RRSP you have now, you are generally able to transfer it to another RRSP with another issuer.

The funds in the RRSP must be transferred directly between issuers to avoid being taxed — you cannot receive the funds personally. The new RRSP issuer will provide you with the appropriate form for the transfer. Bear in mind that you might not be able to transfer some guaranteed investments until maturity, or if you are able to, penalties may apply. In the step-by-step RRSP program outlined in Chapter 4, you will eventually transfer your depository RRSPs to one self-directed trusteed type of RRSP.

It also might be possible to transfer amounts in your RRSP to the pension plan you belong to at your workplace. You might consider doing this if your pension plan were being upgraded and you had to supply a portion of the costs of the upgrade while your employer paid for the rest.

RRSPs — the Great Inflation Fighter

Now that inflation seems to be under control, Canadians are not as worried about their savings losing their purchasing power. But that is no reason to be complacent about the earnings in your RRSP.

If your wages were to increase at exactly the inflation rate each year, you would be no further ahead year after year. Assuming the same proportion of your wages was still taxed, you would only be able to afford to pay for the same basket of groceries, to pay the same rent, to buy the same amount of clothing, and to take the same type of vacations. Similarly, if your RRSP only keeps pace with inflation, every dollar you contribute will have exactly the same spending power during your retirement as those dollars do today. Harking back to the first paragraph of this book, you would have to earn twice as much this year if you expected to support yourself and your family for 24 months — 12 months now and 12 months when you are retired.

Low investment returns and taxes are the two culprits that conspire to make you more vulnerable to the effects of inflation. Canadians traditionally have opted for safe, secure investments that pay a low rate of interest. However, historically, short-term interest rates, which are those paid on savings accounts or 30- to 90-day term deposits or Government-issued treasury bills (T-bills), have only just managed to keep pace with the inflation rate. And after paying tax on this interest, your investment return is less than the inflation rate. *You can actually end up falling be-*

hind. In other words, after redeeming your investments, your dollars will buy a smaller cart of groceries than they would have before you invested.

How do you ensure that you are further ahead when you finally retire? The step-by-step RRSP program and the very nature of RRSPs combine to come to your rescue. The program outlines a basic investment program stressing the use of investment funds over the long term. Historically, this method of investing has provided an attractive return that has outstripped inflation by a wide margin.

And as pointed out several years ago by Sid Himmel, a chartered accountant writing in the *Financial Post*, RRSPs actually eliminate tax on the income earned on the *net amount* invested. This net amount is simply the amount contributed minus the amount by which your taxes are reduced. Or looked at another way, the net amount invested is the after-tax amount that you are able to invest outside an RRSP since no tax deduction is available.

Looking back at the example in Chapter 1, you will remember that you had a choice of investing $600 of after-tax funds in a savings account paying five per cent or making an RRSP investment that also earned five per cent. Since your marginal tax rate is 40 per cent, you could invest $1,000 in the RRSP, which produces a $400 tax refund. In effect you have invested the after-tax amount of $600 in the RRSP plus the $400 tax refund.

At the end of one year, your savings account has grown to $630, consisting of the $600 invested plus $30 of interest earned at five per cent. This $30 is subject to tax.

The RRSP has grown to $1,050 at the end of one year, consisting of the original $1,000 invested, plus $50 of interest earned at five per cent. If you cancel the RRSP at this point, tax must be paid on the whole amount. If your tax rate is still 40 per cent, tax of $420 is paid (40 per cent of $1,050), leaving you with $630 ($1,050 minus $420), the same amount that you earned outside the RRSP before taxes. Thus, there is no tax on the earnings on your net investment in the RRSP ($30 of interest earned at five per cent on $600). The Government's share of your contribution (the $400 tax reduction) and the income earned on this $400 pay any taxes when you cancel the RRSP.

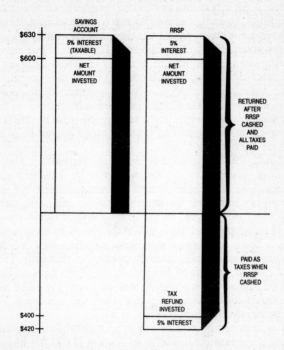

Figure 2.1
RRSPS Eliminate Tax on the Earnings on Your Net Investment

The fact that *RRSPs eliminate tax on your net investment income* applies no matter how much you invest, how much your RRSP earns, or how long you hold your RRSP — just as long as your tax rate does not increase. If your tax rate decreases, which it may after you retire, you will actually get some of your tax dollars back. In other words, the Government may actually provide some of your retirement income. Remember that tax is payable on all RRSP amounts received, but you probably will not begin receiving RRSP income until you are retired.

This concept is extremely important to bear in mind when you are comparing investments and deciding whether or not to invest in an RRSP. Assuming that your tax rate does not increase, there is no other investment vehicle that eliminates tax no matter how much you earn. Yes, you can earn up to $100,000 of tax-exempt capital gains over your lifetime, but many Canadians will eventually exceed this limit. For example, if you now own a vacation home, it won't be too many years before your gain, which is taxable, exceeds $100,000. Capital gains are taxed more heavily now than they were in past years. And remember that the $1,000 investment income deduction, which exempted interest income from tax, has been eliminated.

As well, RRSPs accentuate the *magic of compounding*. Compounding simply means that the earnings on an investment are reinvested, so that, in effect, interest is earned on interest. Not all investments compound the same way. Some compound each year, after taxes are paid on the annual earnings. Others compound before tax, since tax is paid at the end of the investment period. Some investments compound annually, while others compound semi-annually, quarterly, monthly, or even daily. The more often an investment compounds, the higher the earnings over the particular time period. As well, the longer you hold your investments and the higher the rate of return, the more beneficial will be the effects of compounding.

How important is compounding in your RRSP? Recalling the results of the example from Chapter 1 where $1,000 was invested in the RRSP and $600 in a savings account outside an RRSP, about $2,600 was accumulated in the RRSP after tax, while only about $1,450 was accumulated outside after 30 years. Since RRSPs eliminate tax on your net investment income and earnings in the RRSP are not taxed, it is evident that compounding works much more effectively inside an RRSP than outside. If we double the rate of interest earned to 10 per cent, the magic of compounding enhances the RRSP even more. Outside the RRSP, about $3,450 will accumulate. However, by using the RRSP, you accumulate almost $10,500 after taxes — almost three times as much. And if the investment is held for 40 years instead of 30 years, over four times as much will be accumulated with the RRSP.

How Much Better Off Will You Be With an RRSP?

Figure 2.2 shows how four different investments grow over a period of 30 years after all taxes have been levied. The same net investment of $600 (total investment of $1,000 to RRSPs) is made in each. It is assumed that the inflation rate averages five per cent over this period. It is also assumed that all investment income compounds annually, that is, the investment income is reinvested at the end of each year, even though it may have been earned or received at various points during the year.

Investment A is a savings account that earns interest at five per cent which is taxed at your marginal tax rate of 40 per cent. Since your after-tax income is only three per cent annually, you will fall further and further behind inflation every year. In fact, if that $600 will buy five shopping carts full of groceries now, your savings account will be able to buy only three shopping carts of groceries in 30 years.

Investment B is also an interest-bearing security, perhaps a series of one- or two-year GICs or maybe Canada Savings Bonds. The interest rate averages 7.5 per cent but this interest income is also taxable each year at the rate of 40 per cent. If you put your money into investment B, you would still lose ground against inflation over the 30-year period. After paying tax, your after-tax return each year is only 4.5 per cent, a full half a percentage point lower than the inflation rate. Even though you have done a little better than with the savings account, you are still not winning the battle.

Investment C is the same security as Investment B with interest at 7.5 per cent, but this time it is held in an RRSP. Your net investment in the RRSP (after allowing for your tax reduction) is the same as the amount invested in A or B. Since RRSPs eliminate tax on the income on your net investment, you are much better off than with Investment B. You are also better off than with Investment A, because your return is 2.5 percentage points higher.

Investment D is a mutual fund that invests primarily in the stock market (an equity fund). It is also held in your RRSP. The net amount invested is the same as Investments A, B, and C. The earnings rate is 15 per cent. Over 20 investment funds eligible for RRSPs have earned at least this much on average over the last

10 years. With this investment, you are much better off than with any of the other three. In fact, at the end of 30 years, you have over seven times as much accumulated after taxes than is accumulated with Investment C. And you are over 25 times better off than with the savings account.

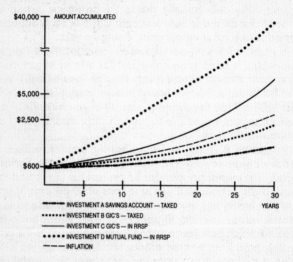

Figure 2.2
You Are Much Better Off Investing With an RRSP

The amount accumulated with Investment D seems quite high. In fact, if you contribute $2,000 or $3,000 each year to an RRSP for 30 years, you should accumulate well over a million dollars, perhaps even over two million dollars. But do not forget that these are dollars that will be spent 30 years from now. These are not the same dollars that you spend today. Actually, with an inflation rate of five per cent, you will need about $4.30 in 30 years time to purchase what $1.00 will buy today.

It is a good idea to think of amounts accumulated in your RRSP in terms of today's dollars — that is, what $1.00 will buy today, not what it might buy in the future. For example, after allowing for inflation, which averages five per cent, you will accumulate about $9,200 with Investment D, expressed in terms of today's dollars. By measuring the amount accumulated in today's dollars, the assumption is made that there is zero inflation, which simply means that $600 will buy the same basket of goods now and at any point in the future. Thus, the purchasing power of the $600 invested increases by over 15 times ($9,200 divided by $600).

CHAPTER THREE

How Much Can You Contribute and Other Essentials

A LONG WITH pension reform (see Appendix B), which is currently being introduced federally and in several provinces, come a number of changes to RRSPs. Some are already law, but the major ones are expected to be introduced in 1991 with several being phased in through to 1995. You are cautioned, however, that the rules explained in this chapter for 1991 and future years are based on Government proposals, not on law, and could therefore change before the new law takes effect.

Perhaps the most significant change, particularly for employees who are members of pension plans, is the promise that Revenue Canada will be telling all taxpayers the maximum that they can contribute to an RRSP in any particular year. Notification will come by mail towards the end of the year beginning in 1991. To some extent, this makes a portion of this chapter redundant. Nevertheless, you still need to know your RRSP contribution limit for 1989 and 1990. More importantly, however, you will be much better off if you know how much you can contribute in 1991, and you do indeed make that contribution, at the beginning of the year rather than at the end. By simply making your RRSP contribution in January of each year instead of waiting until the end of the year or the following January or February, you can increase the size of your RRSP retirement income by as much as 10 per cent or 15 per cent. This and several other techniques for putting more muscle into your RRSP are discussed in Chapter 5.

Who Can Contribute?

Virtually every worker in Canada, employed or self-employed, is eligible to contribute to an RRSP, as long as you are less than 72 years of age. How much you can contribute depends on your *earned income* (a term defined below) and whether or not you are a member of a company pension plan or deferred profit sharing plan. You may contribute to your own RRSP or to your spouse's plan (you *must* be married — unmarried persons living together are not considered to be married for tax and RRSP purposes, even though they may have children). Whether you contribute to your plan or your spouse's, the amount contributed is deductible from your income when you fill out your tax return (contributions remain fully deductible under tax reform). This reduces your taxes, sometimes by thousands of dollars if your contributions are large enough, and for almost all employees results in a tax refund.

You are also permitted to transfer certain pension amounts to your RRSP on a tax-free basis (see below).

How Much Can You Contribute?

The contribution rules for 1989 and 1990 are different from the rules that will apply in 1991 and following years. For 1989 and 1990 contributions, the standard limit is 20 per cent of earned income in the year to a maximum of $7,500. The limit is reduced if you are a member of a company pension plan from which you are entitled to benefits in respect of employment during the year, or a member of a deferred profit sharing plan to which a contribution was made in the year. In this case, the limit is 20 per cent of earned income in 1989 and 1990 to a maximum of $3,500, minus all tax deductions claimed for contributions made by you in the year to the pension plan.

Beginning in 1991, the standard limit (before allowing for company pension plan contributions — see following page) is 18 per cent of your earned income in the immediately preceding year (1990 earned income for a 1991 contribution) to a maximum of a specific dollar amount for that particular year. This yearly maximum is phased in as follows:

1991 $11,500

1992	$12,500
1993	$13,500
1994	$14,500
1995	$15,500

The 1995 limit of $15,500 will be indexed according to increases in the average industrial wage beginning in 1996.

Earned income generally includes:

- employment income (minus union dues, and other deductible expenses of employment);
- income less losses from self-employment or a business in which you are actively engaged;
- royalties received by authors or inventors;
- net research grants;
- net rental income from real estate;
- alimony and maintenance payments received (alimony or maintenance payments that you *make* reduce earned income); and
- most forms of pension income, less amounts transferred on a tax-free basis to your RRSP.

Beginning in 1990, earned income will no longer include pension plan benefits.

If You Belong to a Pension Plan

Beginning in 1991, the RRSP contribution limit for members of pension plans and deferred profit sharing plans (DPSPs) will be calculated differently depending on the type of plan and the amount contributed. There are essentially two different kinds of registered pension plans (RPPs).

Under a *money purchase* registered pension plan (also called a *defined contribution* plan), the employee and usually the employer both contribute to the plan. The best pension possible is then purchased with the accumulated funds in the plan when the employee retires. With a DPSP, a different type of money purchase plan, only the employer generally contributes to the plan (employees are not permitted to contribute to a DPSP after 1989). The RRSP contribution limit for members of either type of plan is the standard limit minus all contributions made in the previous year to the money purchase RPP or DPSP by both the employer and employee. The amount deducted from the standard limit is called the *pension adjustment* (PA).

In 1991, for example, assume that your earned income for RRSP purposes is $32,000 (that is, earned income based on 1990 income). Therefore, your standard RRSP contribution limit is the lesser of $11,500 or 18 per cent of $32,000 = $5,760. In 1990, you contributed $1,000 to your company-sponsored money purchase RPP and your employer contributed $1,200. Thus, you are able to contribute up to $3,560 to your RRSP ($5,760 minus $1,000 minus $1,200). As noted above, you will be advised of your RRSP *contribution room* (the term simply refers to the maximum you are allowed to contribute to an RRSP in any particular year) by Revenue Canada late each year. This figure will take into account total contributions made by you and your employer to any RPP or DPSP. As well, your employer will advise you of your previous year's PA when you receive your T4 slip at the end of February (a T4 details your earnings and tax paid; it must be included with your tax return). If you know your PA, you should be able to determine your RRSP contribution limit.

Members of *defined benefit* registered pension plans also will have a PA that reduces their RRSP contribution limit, but this is calculated in a different manner. Under a defined benefit RPP, a certain pension is guaranteed to be paid at retirement. The employer, with or without the financial help of the employee, provides the necessary funding to ensure the required pension is indeed paid. Over 90 per cent of Canadian workers with pension plans are covered by defined benefit plans.

The PA for members of defined benefit RPPs is based on the benefits payable under the terms of the plan. For example, assume again that your earned income is $32,000, but you are a member of a defined benefit plan that pays 40 per cent of the maximum pension allowed under the law (few plans pay the maximum pension). In general terms, your standard RRSP contribution limit is reduced by 40 per cent, but since not all pension plans are the same, you are permitted to contribute an extra $600 to your RRSP. Thus, you can contribute up to $4,056 to your RRSP in 1989 ($5,760 minus $2,304 — 40 per cent of $5,760 — plus $600).

The actual calculation will be considerably more difficult, depending on the exact terms of your pension plan. However, remember that late each year Revenue Canada will tell you the maximum you can contribute to your RRSP (contribution room) and your employer will notify you of your PA. This figure will take into account the PA for members of defined benefit RPPs. Further details on calculating the defined benefit plan PA are contained in Appendix B.

Additional voluntary contributions (AVCs) made to a pension plan will not be deductible after 1989. Such voluntary saving must be done through an RRSP to obtain a tax deduction.

When Can You Contribute?

Contributions made to an RRSP during the first 60 days of a year are deductible for either that year or the preceding year. Thus, if you contribute on March 1, 1990, you may deduct any portion of the amount on either your 1989 or 1990 tax return. The portion not deducted in 1989 is deductible in 1990.

As explained in Chapter 6, you should attempt to make your RRSP contributions as early in the year as possible. Unfortunately, if you belong to a pension plan or DPSP, it will not be easy to determine exactly the maximum that you are eligible to contribute for 1991 until at least the end of February. If you want to contribute earlier, and you should, consider enlisting the aid of your employer, who should be able to give you a rough approximation of the maximum you can contribute. For example, your employer should be able to tell you to contribute no more than, say, 45 per cent of your standard RRSP limit because your RPP provides about 55 per cent of the maximum benefits. Considering the $600 extra you are allowed to contribute if you are a member of a defined benefit plan, you will probably err on the side of safety. Later in the year, you will be able to make up whatever extra you are eligible to contribute.

Seven-Year Carry Forward of RRSP Contribution Room

One change all RRSP contributors will welcome is the seven year carry forward. Unfortunately, this change does not apply in 1989 or 1990. In any year, beginning in 1991, that you do not make a maximum contribution to your RRSP within your annual limit, you may carry forward this unused contribution room to any of the next seven years.

For example, assume that in 1991 you contribute only $2,000 instead of the maximum $4,000 that you are allowed. In any year from 1992 to 1998 inclusive, you may contribute that $2,000 and claim a tax deduction in the year you actually make the contribution (actually, you will have until 60 days after the end of 1998 to make up for the $2,000 not contributed). Assume further that in 1992, your total contribution room is $5,000, consisting of $2,000 carried forward from 1991 and $3,000 from 1992, the current year. You contribute $3,500 to your RRSP. In this case, $2,000 of the $3,500 contributed is applied against the 1991 carry forward, and you are allowed to carry forward $1,500 ($5,000 minus $3,500) in respect of 1992 for the next seven years.

This provision is particularly valuable for persons just entering the work force who usually do not have the funds to make a maximum contribution, for those who are faced with large expenditures such as the down payment on a home, and for those who plan to be out of the work force for a period of time and do not have the funds available for a large contribution.

However, you should not get in the habit of delaying your RRSP contribution, figuring that you have the next seven years to make it up. First, you will be much better off with your funds inside the RRSP than outside. Second, you may not have the cash available in a year or two to make up for all your contribution room available.

Note that interest paid on loans used to finance an RRSP contribution is not tax-deductible. Therefore, without the tax saving it can be very expensive to borrow to make that large contribution after a few years.

Bear in mind that there is no carry forward if you do not make the maximum contribution for 1989 and 1990 — the new rule takes effect for 1991 contributions. Thus, it might be worthwhile borrowing over the short term (no longer than a year or two) to make maximum contributions in 1989 and 1990. If a portion of the loan remains outstanding in 1991 or 1992, you might consider delaying your RRSP contribution and take advantage of the carry-forward provisions in order to generate the cash to pay off the debt.

Contributing Too Much to Your RRSP

Penalties may apply if you contribute more to your RRSP than your eligible contribution room. Beginning in 1991, however, you are allowed an $8,000 cumulative cushion; in other words, at any point in time you are permitted to have made excess contributions totalling no more than $8,000 that have not been deducted from income. You may deduct these amounts from income in any future year, within your regular contribution limits, and they will no longer be considered excess contributions. Persons under 18 will not be permitted to have an excess amount contributed to their RRSPs.

Any excess amount contributed above $8,000 is subject to a penalty of 1 per cent a month for each month the offending amount remains in your RRSP. This amount may have to be included in income when withdrawn from your RRSP, which results in another extremely severe penalty. However, since you will be informed of your total contribution limit by Revenue Canada each year, there is certainly no excuse for making excess contributions above the $8,000 cushion.

An excess contribution below the $8,000 limit is taxable when it is eventually withdrawn. In effect you are being taxed twice on the same income since you did not receive a deduction for the excess contribution to your RRSP. It will obviously be to your benefit to claim a deduction for such an excess amount in a later year.

Nevertheless, a case can be made for not taking the deduction, if you leave the excess amount in the RRSP for at least 15 or 20 years. In this situation, you may actually be better off than investing it outside your RRSP, because income earned in the RRSP is only taxed when the funds are eventually received, not every year as the income would be if the funds were invested outside the RRSP.

In 1989 and 1990, the excess contribution limit is $5,500. If your actual limit is greater than $5,500 (maximum is $7,500), you may not contribute more than your limit without incurring a penalty.

Arranging for a Retirement Income

You are not allowed to have an RRSP beyond December 31 of the year you turn age 71. On or before that date, you must have arranged to begin receiving a retirement income to be generated by the amounts accumulated in your RRSPs. There are a variety of RRSP retirement income options to choose from.

If you neglect to arrange a retirement income by this date with any of your RRSPs, the entire amount in those RRSPs will be included in your income for tax purposes in the following year, and you will likely pay tax on most of it at rates as high as 50 per cent. Your RRSP may provide for automatic maturity (the term given to arranging for a retirement income), but there is every possibility that the option chosen will not suit your needs.

Choosing the most suitable and best retirement income is extremely important — you may have to live with some choices you make for 20 or 30 or more years. Don't wait until the last minute, and don't make your decisions hastily. After all, you may have been saving and planning for 30 or 40 years. Why not continue to get the most out of your RRSPs? Retirement income planning with your RRSP is discussed in Chapter 7.

Employer-Related or Group RRSPs

Some organizations have RRSP arrangements under which an amount is deducted from your wages and contributed to an RRSP on your behalf (often called group RRSPs). In this situation, the RRSP may operate like a pension plan. These contributions may be locked-in, which means that you cannot cancel the plan to gain access to the funds while you are still involved with the organization and perhaps even after your involvement ceases. However, you should be able to arrange for a retirement income from such an RRSP before normal retirement age. The advantage of a group RRSP is that your contributions are deducted from your wages and therefore you receive the tax benefits immediately. As well, your plan is fully portable, that is, everything goes with you if you change jobs. In many plans, the employee can control how contributions are invested.

Transfer of Pension Benefits to an RRSP

Up to and including 1989, you are allowed to transfer, on a tax-free basis, a variety of pension benefits that you receive periodically to your RRSP. Lump-sum pension amounts must be

transferred to your RRSP directly. Normally, such amounts
would be included in your income and be subject to tax. Such
amounts can be received directly by you, but to qualify for the
tax-free transfer, they must be deposited to your RRSP within 60
days after the end of the year (by March 1, 1990). Technically,
the entire amount is included in your income on your tax return
and you are allowed a deduction for the amount deposited to
your RRSP up to the amount originally received. Such amounts
include:

* any amount received periodically from a registered pension
  plan;
* any taxable amount received periodically from a DPSP;
* amounts received under the Old Age Security Plan or Canada
  Pension Plan or similar payments from a provincial plan;
* amounts received as a retiring allowance, but limited to $2,000
  for each year of service with the employer plus $1,500 for
  each year that you were not covered by a pension plan with
  that employer before 1989; and
* amounts received as retirement income from an RRSP, including commuted annuity amounts and amounts received from a
  registered retirement income fund (RRIF — see Chapter 7) in
  excess of the mandatory minimum annual payment.

Beginning in 1990, only lump-sum RPP amounts, lump-sum
taxable DPSP benefits, retiring allowances, and commuted RRSP
annuity and RRIF amounts in excess of the mandatory minimum
annual payment may be transferred on a tax-free basis to your
RRSP. Except for retiring allowances, these transfers must be
made directly between plans. From 1989 to 1994 inclusive, you
may make a tax-free transfer of up to $6,000 of RPP benefits a
year to a spousal RRSP.

Special Situations

The RRSP rules are complex and far-reaching, covering a huge
variety of situations, many having to do with the abuse of RRSP
privileges. Three special situations that may affect Canadians are
discussed briefly in Appendix C: marriage breakdown, death, and
emigration from Canada.

CHAPTER FOUR

Step-by-Step RRSP Program

B Y ANYONE'S definition, a worry-free RRSP is one that takes up hardly any of your time, demands virtually nothing from you in the way of investment or technical expertise, promises to provide an attractive retirement income, and, above all, lets you sleep contentedly at night.

The step-by-step guide to a worry-free RRSP outlined in this chapter fits this definition like a glove. The program shows you how to invest each dollar you are able to contribute each year. Once you understand the program, your RRSP should take up no more than an hour or two of your time each year. Only three common types of investments are used — Canada Savings Bonds, money market investment funds, and equity investment funds (the latter two are often called mutual funds). Combined, they have a strong history of providing, on average, attractive but secure gains over the long term. And the more you accumulate in your RRSP, the larger your retirement income will eventually be. With both types of investment funds, you get professional management and do not have to rely on your own limited experience. You simply pick the best funds based on their performance over the past few years.

The most difficult step to take in the program is finding the cash each year to make your contribution (see Chapter 2). Once this has been accomplished, however, you simply assess where you stand — that is, how many years away from retiring you are and how much in total you, or you and your spouse, have already contributed to your RRSPs. Then you make the appropriate RRSP investments with your current contribution. After a few years, this may be as easy as writing one cheque and making one five-minute phone call. For the first few years, you will have to decide which mutual funds to invest in (each month they are ranked according to performance over various periods, including the last year and the preceding ten years, which makes it relatively easy to decide). And every year you should review the performance of your investments at least once (this should take only a few minutes) to ensure they are doing as well as you expect.

Some people like to spend more time with their investments. This may lead to slightly better average returns, but it also may not. Bear in mind that an expert, particularly in the investment field, is someone who is right more often than most other people — but that person is still not right all the time. Amateur investors are, by definition, wrong more often than professionals. If you manage to buy and sell at the wrong time often enough, your average return over the long term could be much lower than someone who rigorously sticks to a program of investing in mutual funds and lets a professional make the decisions.

You Only Need Three Investments

The three investments that you will use in the program are outlined briefly here. More detail is provided in Appendix A, including tips on how to narrow down your choice of investment funds to buy.

Money Market Funds.   These invest in short-term securities, most of which are government guaranteed, such as Treasury Bills. With your RRSP contribution, you purchase units (also called shares) in the fund. Your units are registered as an RRSP investment. The interest income (and occasionally capital gains) earned by the fund is generally credited to you weekly. The rate of return that you earn varies depending on interest rates earned on investments that are owned by the fund. You can open a money market fund RRSP with as little as $500 and make further contributions of as little as $100. Most money market fund RRSPs do not charge a commission on the purchase or sale of units (do not buy into a fund that does), and the monthly administration charge (this pays the funds expenses and provides for a profit for the fund's administrator) is generally quite small. You will be charged an initial fee for registering your units as an RRSP investment.

Canada Savings Bonds (CSBs). Most Canadians have owned CSBs at one time or another, primarily because they are risk-free, convenient and very flexible. They are available each year in late October and early November in denominations as small as $100. They carry an interest rate that is usually comparable to the rate paid on money market funds at that time. However, this rate is guaranteed for one year. There are two types of CSBs — compound interest and those which pay interest annually. CSBs generally mature in seven years. Unlike other bonds, CSBs can be cashed at any time for their face value plus all interest owing to the end of the preceding month (interest is not payable if you cash them within three months of purchase). As an RRSP investment, CSBs can only be purchased through a self-directed RRSP.

Equity Funds — Balanced, Conservative or Aggressive. An equity investment fund is a pool of cash received from a number of taxpayers which is invested by an expert, or group of experts, primarily in shares of public companies listed on a stock exchange. You buy units in the fund. The value of your units depends on the value of the investments held by the fund at any point in time. Your units are registered as an RRSP investment if the fund qualifies as an eligible RRSP investment. A number of funds charge a sales commission on purchase (often called a front-end load) and others charge a fee if you sell your units. All funds charge a management or administration fee, and you will probably be charged a small fee initially and then annually for registering and maintaining your units as an RRSP investment. Equity funds take different investment approaches. Some may invest aggressively and look mostly for capital gains. Others may invest more conservatively and look for both capital gains and a reasonable level of dividend income. Still others, called balanced funds, invest in both shares and interest-bearing securities, weighting their holdings of one or the other more heavily depending on where they think the stock market and interest rates are heading. Another type of equity fund invests primarily in foreign shares. Units of this type can only be held in a self-directed RRSP within specific limits.

Aren't Equity Funds Too Risky Since They Invest in the Stock Market?

Yes, there is an element of risk attached to equity funds, but if you want to eventually achieve a reasonable level of financial security, you must be prepared to accept a reasonable degree of risk.

All investments contain an element of risk. Canada Savings Bonds are risk-free from the point of view of your investment being secure and interest at the stated rate being paid (the federal government guarantees that interest will be paid and that you will receive your invested capital back on maturity of the CSB). However, there is no guarantee that you will do better than inflation, especially after you have paid tax on the interest. This means that by buying Canada Savings Bonds, supposedly the safest of investments, you may be no better off after seven or eight years. With a Guaranteed Investment Certificate (GIC) where you are locked-in to the stated interest rate for, say, five years, and it is difficult and probably costly to sell the investment, there is even more risk that you could fall behind inflation. That is why a five-year GIC carries a higher interest rate than a Canada Savings Bond.

You have every right to question the quality of an "investment" where you just break even. If a "risk-free" investment leaves you in the same place from which you started, perhaps you should be thinking of a different way to invest your money.

An equity fund investment, on the other hand, is without a doubt "less secure" than a CSB. If there is a downturn in the stock market, your investment could be worth less than what you paid. There is also no guarantee that your investment will earn 10 or 15 or 20 per cent every year, whereas you are guaranteed a minimum rate with the CSB until maturity. However, *over the long term*, equity funds have outperformed CSBs and GICs by a wide margin. If you hold on to your equity fund investment over the long term (at least seven or eight and preferably 10 or more years), you should be rewarded with an attractive return if history repeats itself. Thus, if you are willing to put up with less security on your invested capital, with no guarantee that you will earn a positive return, and you hold the investment for the long term and rely on history repeating itself (all of which means accepting more risk), you should do better with the equity fund than with the CSB or GIC. There is no absolute guarantee that you will — that is what risk is all about — but the odds are definitely in your favour.

You might want to compare buying an equity fund to buying a house. After you have invested your $10,000 or $20,000 or $30,000, house prices may decline drastically, as they did in the West recently. In fact, in small, one-industry towns, your house could prove to be worthless. Or you may find yourself having to renew your nine per cent mortgage at 18 per cent after a year. Or you might discover that you bought a lemon, or the builder goes bankrupt before your home is finished. Any number of disasters can happen. When examined from all sides, there is no denying that a house is a more risky investment than a Canada Savings Bond. But to the huge majority of Canadians, a house has been and continues to be the best investment they have made and will ever make.

Similarly, history has proved that over the last 20 or 25 years investment funds are good investments which can keep you well ahead of inflation, despite the risk. In fact, the longer you plan to hold on to your equity funds, the lower the risk becomes.

So, you are probably asking, what about the October 1987 stock market "crash"? The stock market does indeed take a dive every once in a while. In this case it went down a lot in one day, but it has since recovered much of its loss. In fact, the stock market broke about even in 1987 and had made substantial gains by mid-1989. At least two dozen popular equity funds have had average annual gains of 14 per cent or better the last five years, while money market funds gained only about 9 per cent. Over half a dozen equity funds have done better than 16 per cent over the last ten years. These periods include October 1987.

Remember, you are investing for the long term. The market goes down and the market goes up, but over the long term the direction has been inexorably up. There is no reason on the horizon why history will not continue to repeat itself.

Why These Three Investments and Not Others?

The most common RRSP investment — shorter-term Guaranteed Investment Certificates (GICs) and term deposits with maturities up to five years — do not put your dollars to work for you as hard as they really should be working. In fact, this type of investment can actually be dangerous at times. If you buy a five-year GIC at eight per cent and six months later inflation has climbed to 14 per cent where it stays for the next four-and-a-half years, your investment will have much less purchasing power on maturity than it had when originally purchased. The opposite is true, of course, when the inflation rate and interest rates are declining.

You can reduce the risk associated with GICs by purchasing a five-year GIC each and every year with your RRSP contribution. This is called dollar cost averaging, which is simply the process of buying a series of investments according to a fixed schedule, such as every month or every year, and ignoring current interest rates or stock market conditions. However, at any point in time, all of your funds are locked-in for up to five years. In later years, these locked-in amounts could be substantial. You also must reinvest RRSP funds each year, although you would normally just purchase another five-year GIC.

Your primary investment goal with your RRSP is to accumulate as much money as possible with a minimum of risk. This will get you as far ahead of inflation as possible. History has shown that over the past six decades, short-term interest rates (those available with money market funds) have just kept pace with inflation. Over the last ten years, they have been about two percentage points higher than inflation, but only because interest rates and inflation have been so volatile.

Longer-term interest rates have managed to outperform inflation by only one-half to a full percentage point over the last 60 years. This is not enough to pull you well ahead of inflation over the limited number of years that you can contribute to your RRSP. Hence, fixed-income investment funds, which invest primarily in bonds, mortgages, and other interest-bearing securities, are ignored for your RRSP. They are, however, a good investment later when you are arranging your retirement income because the protection of your accumulated funds is stressed more than growth.

The stock market, and hence equity funds which invest primarily in the stock market, have outperformed inflation by six to eight percentage points. The better equity funds have managed an eight to 12 percentage point annual gain on inflation over the last 10 years.

If you can combine the three investments to get a return of from eight to 10 percentage points on average above the average inflation rate, you are doing well, and will not be disappointed when you arrange a retirement income with your RRSP. In mid-1988, the inflation rate was still at about four per cent, which means that you would want an average return of 12 per cent to 14 per cent. Many of the RRSP-eligible equity funds have earned more than 14 per cent on average over the past ten years, and several have earned more than 17 per cent. Money market funds are earning about 10 per cent in mid-1989, and the 1988 CSB issue went for nine and a half per cent. Thus, if 25 per cent of your RRSP were in money market funds and 75 per cent in an equity fund earning 15 per cent, you would have a combined return of more than 13 per cent.

Please note that here and elsewhere in the text, the percentage returns quoted on RRSP investments are based on historical earnings, particularly those of the last ten years. *There is no guarantee that history will repeat itself.* The history of investment returns indicates that you should do as well in the next ten years as you would have over the past ten years (that is, the return on various investments should be a certain number of percentage points above the inflation rate), but there is always the chance that this may not be the case. You stand a better chance of success, however, if you invest with the long term in mind and let history run its course, and if you use mutual funds and let the professionals make investment decisions for you. They are well-qualified to protect your investments in the event of historical change from the norm and will adapt accordingly. Can you say the same thing if you decide to invest in safe, secure GICs? If there is significant change, will you have any idea how to reinvest your GIC funds, assuming you end up with much of anything?

Why Combine the Three Investments?

One obvious question you might have is why not invest everything in the equity fund that earns 15 per cent, instead of settling for 13 per cent? In a word, the answer is *insurance*.

Not everyone manages to keep their RRSPs intact until they
retire. If you have some type of financial emergency, you might
have to get your hands on cash quickly. CSBs and money market
funds can be redeemed very quickly, and you do not have to
worry about selling them at an inopportune time. Your investment in an equity fund can also generally be redeemed quickly,
but it may be the wrong time to sell. For example, you may have
bought your equity fund units last year, but they have declined in
value by 10 per cent. You have confidence that if you hold onto
them, history will take its course and they will appreciate significantly in value over the next few years. At this point you would
be much better off selling units in your money market fund or
some of your CSBs.

In fact, many Canadians hold their emergency funds inside
their RRSPs. If you recall, there is no tax on the income
earned on your net RRSP investment. Since investment income
earned outside your RRSP is subject to tax, you will be better
off investing your emergency funds inside your RRSP. With
any luck, you won't have to touch these emergency funds and
you will have that much more in your RRSP to finance your
retirement.

As well, not everyone has the same tolerance to risk. Many
Canadians will want at least 25 per cent of their RRSP invested
in low-risk money market funds or CSBs and take the consequences of a lower return over the long term. They just sleep
better at night. Others will fine tune their tolerance to risk by
varying the composition of their equity fund investing. For example, those who do not like much risk may invest primarily
in balanced funds, while others may invest mostly in aggressive equity funds that vary in value considerably, even from
day to day.

Making Your RRSP Investing Worry-Free

The easiest way to start making your RRSP worry-free is to establish an investing schedule and stick to it. For example, if you
and your spouse have decided that you both can contribute $400
a month in total to your RRSPs, arrange to have it automatically
withdrawn from your bank accounts. You might contribute $100
to a money market fund and $100 to each of three different eq-

uity funds. You make the equity fund investments whether the market is up or down — it just happens automatically at the beginning of every month.

This method of investing is called *dollar cost averaging.* Rather than trying to predict when the market is low so you can do all your buying at that point, you ignore what the market is doing. The times that you buy in when the market is high and poised to drop are balanced against the times that you buy when the market is at its lowest and set to rise. In other words, you rely on long-term historical trends. You also save a lot of wear and tear on the anxiety side of your ledger.

It does not matter when you invest in money market funds since you are earning interest income at short-term rates. In fact, you will usually want to *park* your money in a money market fund, rather than a savings account, when you are waiting to buy Canada Savings Bonds at the end of October.

Where Do You Buy the Three Investments?

You can buy Canada Savings Bonds practically anywhere. However, since they can only be held in a self-directed RRSP, you will eventually buy them from the issuer or administrator of your plan. More on this later.

If you have never purchased units in an investment fund, don't worry — it's just as easy as buying Canada Savings Bonds. The form that you initially fill out asks for the standard information — name, address, social insurance number — and it may ask for details on your employer, your net worth, your investment experience, and investing objectives. As well, it asks you to name a beneficiary for your RRSP should you die. If you choose not to name one, the beneficiaries named in your Will receive amounts in your RRSP.

Many investment funds are billion-dollar operations that have been around for decades. In fact, if you have a pension plan at work, the same people who manage its investments just might manage the mutual fund in which you choose to invest.

Money market funds can be purchased directly from the fund itself, through a broker, or perhaps through your banker or even through independent investment counsellors and financial planners.

Most money market funds and equity funds are members of the Investment Funds Institute. Write to the Institute for the addresses of the various funds, if the ones you like do not have a local telephone listing, and then write to the funds themselves for details and application forms. The address of the Investment Funds Institute is:

>The Investment Funds Institute of Canada
>70 Bond Street
>Suite 400
>Toronto, Ontario
>M5B 1X2
>Telephone 416-363-2158

More detail on money market funds and equity funds is provided in Appendix A, including the names and addresses of some of the larger funds that are not members of the Investment Funds Institute.

Equity funds may be purchased from or through the same sources as money market funds. Several banks and many trust companies offer their own funds. However, many brokers and other members of the financial community may be unwilling to handle no-load funds, that is, funds that have neither a front-end load nor a redemption fee, since these fees represent the seller's commission or profit on the transaction. Thus, no-load funds are usually available from the fund itself.

You might be able to purchase funds with a load from the fund itself, but they will usually charge you the maximum commission, which is often as high as nine per cent. Most often, however, they will refer you to your broker. Brokers and other financial entities generally charge smaller commissions. For example, a full service broker may charge you five per cent on a $5,000 purchase, while a discount broker may charge you as little as three or four per cent. Shop around. If you have never dealt with a broker before, rest assured — they are very accommodating and welcome your business. While banks (which include trust companies, credit unions, etc.) generally do not advertise the fact, many bank managers will help you make your purchase. Make sure that your bank charges no higher a commission than a broker would charge.

If you have not arranged for contributions to an investment fund to be withdrawn automatically from your savings account, you will simply write a cheque for your contribution in succeeding years.

The Step-by-Step Program

The specific investments you buy with your RRSP contribution each year depend on your age, that is, how far away from retiring you are, and the total amount you have contributed to RRSPs to date. If you are married, you can consider the total amount contributed by both you and your spouse, although this isn't absolutely necessary if you are both following the program. It is better to consider both RRSPs together to ensure that the total increase in value each year is meeting both your expectations. You also want to ensure that sufficient cash is invested in money market funds or Canada Savings Bonds to provide what you both consider to be a comfortable cushion for emergencies, while taking into account any investments you both have outside your RRSPs.

Some couples prefer to keep their finances completely separate from each other, often because they think they are preparing themselves for the possibility of divorce. However, you should bear in mind that the family law in most provinces provides for an equal sharing of the value of most assets, including RRSPs, on the permanent breakdown of a marriage.

The step-by-step program has only two goals — contribute as much as you can to your RRSP and accumulate as much as you can. Don't fall into the trap of setting a goal such as accumulating a million dollars in 35 years. To do this, you only have to contribute $14,000 today if your RRSP can earn 13 per cent compounded annually. But what if inflation averages 13 per cent over this period? Your million will still be worth exactly $14,000 in 35 years and you could be looking forward to a bleak retirement. The future is uncertain, so accumulate as much as you possibly can in your RRSP. If you are within a few years of retiring and discover that you have more than enough, celebrate. But before you do, make sure that it is really more than enough. In fact, spending the first few hundred dollars of your celebration money on professional financial advice could be one of the better investments you will make.

Early and Middle Working Years

This period encompasses the bulk of your working life — from the year you get your first job and make your first contribution to an RRSP because you have earned income, to the point where you are about ten years away from retiring. It is assumed in the step-by-step program that you will be arranging a retirement income with your RRSP funds in the year that you retire. If you will have adequate pension income from other sources and do not have to touch your RRSP, consider your retiring date for RRSP purposes to be the year you turn age 71, at which point you must mature your RRSPs (that is, arrange for a retirement income).

It is not necessary that you contribute a specific amount each year to keep up with the program. You simply contribute as much as you can in the year. Finding the cash for your annual contribution was discussed in Chapter 2. As is discussed in more detail in Chapter 5, you should do your utmost to contribute as much as possible each year and to contribute as early in the year as possible. And you should begin contributing as early as possible in your working life. The results can be dramatic. For example, do you realize that if you make a regular contribution of $1,000 to your RRSP from age 25 to 32 (eight years) and then stop contributing, you will accumulate more in your RRSP by age 65 than if you contribute every year for 32 years beginning at age 33?

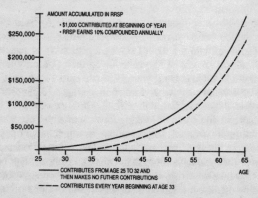

Figure 4.1
Begin Contributing to Your RRSP as Soon as You Can

The First $5,000 You Contribute

This is your cushion in case financial disaster strikes and you need your RRSP funds in a hurry. Contribute the $5,000 to a money market fund. It makes no difference whether you can contribute the full $5,000 in one year or it takes you three or four years.

Tips on choosing a *good* money market fund are presented in Appendix A. If your fund is large and it is with a well-established management group in the investment fund field, you need only one. Some funds perform a little better than others on average, but only a little. Choose one that suits your needs — not all will arrange for automatic deposits.

If you already have one or more RRSPs that are not invested in money market funds, consider switching over as much as you can up to the $5,000 level. If you can transfer the funds this year, go on to the next step in the program with this year's contribution.

To transfer amounts from one RRSP to another, you simply open an RRSP with the money market fund of your choice and fill out the proper form for the transfer. The actual transfer may take up to a month or two — no institution likes losing RRSP dollars. If your existing RRSP is sitting in a savings account type of plan, the transfer will be a simple matter. However, if your old RRSP is in a guaranteed plan, it may be impossible to transfer the amount until the locked-in investment matures. Other guaranteed plans can be transferred, but you will be penalized. For example, assume that you have a five-year deposit that pays 11 per cent if held to maturity. If you cancel it three years early, it may pay only nine per cent for those first two years.

Of course, you should consider a transfer only if you will be earning as much with the money market fund as with the old investment. In the example above, there would be no point in transferring the deposit. You would be sacrificing an 11 per cent return over the last three years for a nine per cent return, and then the money market fund may only be paying seven per cent. When the guaranteed security matures in three years, you would transfer it to one of the three investments depending on how far you have progressed in the step-by-step program. However, if your old RRSP is a savings account type, and therefore earning only four or five per cent, by all means make the transfer as soon as you can.

If you, or you and your spouse, decide that you should have a larger cushion, or emergency fund, increase the size of your contribution to the money market fund at this point. Many financial counsellors suggest that you have three months of before-tax family earnings set aside as an emergency fund invested in something like Canada Savings Bonds or a money market fund. This is good advice, *if you already own your own home.* There is no point in keeping a lot of cash handy for an occasion that may never happen, while you pay rent each month and watch the price of housing steadily march upward. Precious few Canadians regret having put their savings into a down payment on their first home.

Since RRSPs eliminate tax on the earnings on your net investment, and since they are so flexible, you should definitely consider developing your emergency fund in the RRSP. In fact, once your RRSPs begins to grow in value, you may find that having the equivalent of three-month's gross income in low-return money market funds is not necessary.

Finally, if you are already relatively close to retiring, say within 10 or so years, you probably have already figured out how you will cope with any emergencies. Therefore, skip this section and go on to the next — $5,000 to $20,000. You have only a short while to accumulate funds in your RRSP, so you want to get it working as hard as possible for you immediately.

The Next $5,000 to $20,000 That You Contribute

If you have managed to contribute only $500 or $1,000 to your RRSP over the last couple of years, you might think that you have a better chance of winning a lottery than getting up to the $20,000 mark. But take another look at the financial side of your life. Most Canadians can, with a little digging, a little sacrifice, and a dollop of ingenuity, manage to contribute more than they are. Do you realize that the average family income in Canada is about $40,000? Many *average* families are earning $50,000 and even $60,000 if both spouses are working full time. By contributing only 10 per cent of family income to your RRSPs annually (bearing in mind the contribution limits), you can reach $20,000 in four or five years. By the time you and your spouse are in your mid-thirties, you could have contributed well in excess of $50,000. If you both started contributing early enough, you might even have as much as $100,000 in your RRSPs. Anybody in their mid-thirties with $100,000 or more in their RRSPs should be able to look forward to an exceptionally comfortable, almost lavish, retirement — if they continue to contribute.

This next $15,000 is invested in equity funds. To minimize the risk of possibly picking the wrong fund, you should invest in several different funds — three ought to be enough. Not all funds perform the same, although most follow the general direction of the stock market. And some funds consistently perform better than others. By investing in at least three funds you should be able to obtain a good average return. If one of your funds begins to perform poorly for more than two or three years, you can sell it and not be hurt too much by the substandard return.

And by investing specific amounts in at least three different funds, you are able to fine tune your own tolerance to risk. There are essentially four types of RRSP-eligible equity funds:

Balanced Funds. These invest in both stocks and interest-bearing securities depending on the judgment of the manager of the fund. Generally, the manager will weight the fund's investments according to where he or she expects to get the best return while maintaining the total value of the fund. Balanced funds generally do not perform as well as other equity funds over the long term, but they also do not decline in value to the extent equity funds normally do when the stock market drops. In fact, depending on fund management, the value of your investment may not decline at all because the fund has shifted primarily into interest-bearing investments.

Long-term Growth (Lower Variability) Funds. All funds have as their goal long-term growth, but this largest group of equity funds generally does it by investing primarily in solid blue chip stocks that are either thought to be undervalued or have a long history of regularly increasing in value. These long-term growth funds are characterized by not fluctuating in value as widely as aggressive funds, either on daily movements in the stock market or on longer-term movements, whether up or down. In general they have performed almost as well as the aggressive funds over the long term and better than balanced funds. They do not retain their value as well as balanced funds when the stock market is depressed, but they do better than the aggressive funds, which means you will not be greatly disadvantaged if you must cancel your RRSP when the market has declined.

Aggressive Funds. There are only a few funds that can be characterized as aggressive. Large swings in value are characteristic of these funds when the market is fluctuating relatively wildly. With good management, their performance can be outstanding — it can also be miserable, with losses of 20 per cent or 30 per cent not uncommon in bad years. These funds generally stress investing in shares that show the possibility of large gains in value over shorter periods of time. Often the fund manager will invest in industry sectors, such as oil or golds, that he or she feels are due to rebound in the near future and provide substantial gains. In other cases, management may have the same investment philosophy as the growth funds, but because of the choice of investments, the value of the fund swings quite dramatically.

Specialized or Sector Funds. These funds invest exclusively in particular areas, such as real estate, gold, oil and gas, and natural resources. It is recommended that you ignore these as possible investments. One of the goals of the step-by-step RRSP program is to leave all investment decision-making to the professionals. If you decide to invest in a natural resources fund, you are making an investment decision, namely that this sector of the economy will perform as well or better than the economy as a whole. Why not leave this up to the experts? The managers of the other three types of funds cannot help but invest a significant portion of their assets in resources, since this is such a large component of the Canadian economy and at least 90 per cent of their investments must be in companies resident in Canada and listed on a Canadian stock exchange.

The new ethical funds, which do not invest in companies that, for example, have a history of polluting the environment or supporting repressive regimes, are usually classified as either aggressive or long-term growth funds. However, they have only been in existence a short period of time and so far have little in the way of a track record. Hence, it is more risky to invest in these funds than those that have been around for 10 or 15 years.

When you make your first equity fund investments, you may want to minimize risk. Thus, you would invest in a balanced fund that invests in both stocks and interest-bearing securities. Once you gain more experience investing in mutual funds, you may be prepared to take more risk by purchasing units of long-term growth funds or aggressive funds.

Invest this $15,000 in the manner you feel most comfortable. If you are contributing $3,000 a year, you might want to contribute $1,000 to each of three different funds each year. Or you may decide to invest your first $5,000 in a balanced fund, the next $5,000 in a second balanced fund, and the last $5,000 in one or two long-term growth funds. Whichever way you choose to invest, remember to spread your total contributions of $15,000 over at least three funds. By all means invest in four or five funds, but any more is probably not advisable. If you have too many investments, you might not monitor their performance the way you should, and you may end up holding on to a poorly performing fund too long.

Contributions Above the $20,000 Level

Once you reach the $20,000 milestone, you simply begin to add to the investments you have already made in the proportions already established. For example, you should now have investments in at least four different investment funds — three equity funds and a money market fund. If you plan to contribute $4,000, simply write cheques for $1,000 to each of the four funds when it comes time to make your RRSP contribution. Or instruct each fund to withdraw the appropriate amount from your bank account each month, if the funds provide this kind of service. Just remember — for every dollar you contribute to your money market fund, contribute three dollars to your equity funds.

Self-Directed RRSPs

When you have at least $20,000 in your RRSPs, you might want
to consider opening a self-directed plan.

To answer the first two objections you might have — no, self-
directed plans are not just for the well-off or sophisticated investor, and no, they do not have to be risky. They can be just as easy
to use as regular depository RRSPs and can actually solve some
problems that you may run into. You will be under no obligation
to make fancy investment decisions. In fact, you will hold almost
exactly the same investments in the self-directed RRSP as you do
now, except you will now be able to buy Canada Savings Bonds
and a portion of your RRSP can be used to purchase equity funds
that invest internationally, instead of primarily in Canada. Over
the long term, international funds have performed significantly
better than Canadian funds.

There are at least six other reasons for considering a self-
directed RRSP:

1. All your RRSP investments are consolidated under one roof.
   The administrator of your self-directed plan will generally issue monthly reports, detailing purchases, sales, contributions,
   and income earned in the RRSP. This should make it easier to
   monitor your investments.

2. With all your investments in one plan, transfers between investments are much faster and may actually save you money
   in the long term. Purchase and sale orders with a broker, for
   instance, go through the same day. There is no *in transit* time
   when you might have unproductive cash; nor will your cash
   be tied up for an extra week or two in an investment that you
   no longer wish to own. If you cannot immediately decide what
   to do with the cash from the sale of an investment, your self-
   directed RRSP may pay daily interest on cash balances that is
   at least competitive with normal daily interest rates.

3. If you have to withdraw funds from your RRSP, it may be faster with a self-directed plan, since your sale order transactions
   are processed immediately. However, there may be a waiting
   period before your cash is released by brokers. This release

day is called the *settlement date* and is always five business
days after the *transaction date*. If you have your contribution
in a money market fund RRSP, you could probably get your
cash out in a shorter period of time. On the other hand, the
five-day period works to your benefit when making contributions to a self-directed plan. You can make a mutual fund
purchase and not have to provide the cash (that is, your contribution) for five business days, although your purchase takes
effect on the transaction date.

4. When buying investment funds with a front-end load, you will
   save on commissions compared to buying directly from the
   fund itself. The standard commission charged by brokers for
   smaller purchases (up to about $10,000) is five or six per cent,
   compared to up to nine per cent if purchased directly from the
   fund. With larger purchases and larger RRSPs, you may be
   able to negotiate smaller commissions. Discount brokers offer
   even lower commissions — three to five per cent, and even
   less for larger purchases.

5. If you are paying no more than the standard annual administration fee of $100 for your self-directed RRSP, you will do no
   worse than break even and you may even save some money
   compared with having several different RRSPs. Each
   depository RRSP charges either a one-time or an annual administration fee that is cloaked under various names. Most investment funds charge the fee annually and put a ceiling on it,
   perhaps $50 or $75 — it is often calculated as a percentage of
   the value of your units in the fund. This fee is eliminated with
   a self-directed plan. Obviously, if you own units in a number
   of mutual funds, you should come out ahead with the self-
   directed plan. As well, if you pay the annual administration
   fee personally, that is, do not have it deducted from your
   RRSP, the amount is deductible from income for tax purposes.
   Some depository funds also offer this option.

6. If your self-directed RRSP is with a full service broker (not a
   discount broker), you automatically gain access to the broker's
   advice and research. Bear in mind, however, that brokers
   usually allot their time in proportion to the size of a person's

investment portfolio (the term used to describe all a person's investments) and the amount of commissions generated by that person for the broker. If you have a relatively inactive self-directed RRSP, you cannot expect that much time from a broker, although he or she should be able to provide some advice on the several investment funds you are considering buying and the broker will have a few that he or she favours. Discount brokers offer no advice or research — they simply carry out your purchase and sale orders. If you have been happy with your choices of investment funds to date, by all means try using a discount broker and take advantage of the lower commissions and lower annual administration fee.

A self-directed RRSP is a trusteed type of RRSP. Again you will be required to fill in a form and provide basic information about yourself. The administrator of the self-directed plan can then provide the appropriate forms in order to transfer your existing depository RRSPs. You may have to wait until guaranteed investments such as GICs have matured in order to arrange for their transfer.

There is no advantage to maintaining one or two of your existing RRSPs separate from your self-directed plan. First, you lose the benefit of having everything reported by one entity. Second, you will probably pay extra and unnecessary administrative fees. Third, you still gain access to whatever protection your funds had outside your RRSP. For example, the Canada Deposit Insurance protection applies whether, for instance, a bank's GIC is a depository type or is held in a self-directed plan. And fourth, your ability to invest in international investment funds depends on the size of your investments in the self-directed plan, not your total RRSP investments.

RRSP law limits your investments in non-Canadian securities to 10 per cent of the cost of your RRSP investments. However, you can only make the non-Canadian investment in a self-directed plan, and only the cost of the investments in that particular self-directed plan count for purposes of calculating your 10 per cent limit. Thus, if you leave $5,000 invested in a money market fund outside your self-directed RRSP, your ability to invest in an international fund is reduced by $500 (10 per cent of $5,000). Note that this 10 per cent limit is increased if your RRSP makes

qualifying small business investments. These are not recommended in the step-by-step RRSP program.

It is not always easy to determine 10 per cent of the cost of
your investments in order to calculate how many units in an international fund you may purchase. The simplest way to approach the problem is to invest 10 per cent of every contribution.
After you have opened your self-directed plan and have transferred all your RRSP investments into the new plan, simply total up
your contributions in past years and take 10 per cent of this
amount.

However, every so often you will sell an investment fund and
buy another one. And once a year, or perhaps more often, your
investment funds will declare a dividend that will automatically
be reinvested in units of the fund for you. You will also earn interest with your money market fund, which probably will be
reinvested in the fund, and you will earn interest on your Canada
Savings Bonds. All these items add to the cost of your investments and enable you to purchase more units in an international fund. If your self-directed plan is with a full service
broker, you may be able to persuade them to calculate the cost of
your RRSP at any point in time. If not, you will have to keep
track yourself. Having everything reported by one entity will certainly help, but you should try to maintain a running total and
maximize your foreign purchases whenever possible.

You should be prepared to shop around for the self-directed
plan that suits you the best. They are offered by brokers, trust
companies, and several banks. Ensure that you can purchase any
mutual fund (some administrators only allow you to purchase
funds with which they are connected or that offer them the best
commissions) and that you can hold no-load funds in the plan
(some administrators will object because they receive no commission if they make this purchase on your behalf). Ensure that
any cash balances in your plan earn daily interest, and make sure
that the reporting schedule meets your needs. If you like the convenience of having contributions withdrawn directly from your
savings account, make sure that this will be continued and no extra charges will apply. After all this, find out which one of your
choices offers the lowest annual administration fee. Some charge
a flat $100 a year, while others charge according to the number
of transactions with a minimum annual fee.

Contributing $20,000 and More with a Self-Directed RRSP

Now that you have the flexibility of being able to purchase two other types of investments (a large variety of investments actually qualify for self-directed plans), you will want to change your buying habits slightly. First, instead of buying more money market fund units, buy Canada Savings Bonds each October with one quarter of your contribution until you have bought $5,000 worth, the same as your money market fund.

The interest rate on money market funds and CSBs in October is similar, but CSBs have one advantage. If interest rates decline, CSBs will continue to pay the stated rate for one year, whereas the money market fund rate will decline and match current interest rates. If interest rates increase, the money market fund rate will also increase. But so will the rate on CSBs. Since they can be cashed at any time, the Government has been forced to temporarily raise the rate on CSBs to discourage people from cashing them. Thus, while the CSB rate may not rise as quickly as the rate on a money market fund, it will more or less keep pace with short-term interest rates.

If you own CSBs outside your RRSP, you may transfer them to your self-directed plan. This counts as a contribution in the year the transfer is made, and the value of your CSBs at that time, including accrued interest (that is, interest that has been earned but not paid), is deductible from income for tax purposes. However, you are considered to have disposed of the CSBs at the time of transfer and must include the accrued interest in your income for tax purposes.

If you sell capital properties, such as stock or mutual fund investments, to your RRSP, you must recognize any resulting gain for tax purposes in the year of sale. If you realize a loss on the sale, the loss is ignored for tax purposes.

Each year, you should try to put 10 per cent of your contribution into international investment funds. This may not always be possible since most funds require a minimum amount to be invested, even if you already own units in the fund. Thus, when choosing an international fund (you generally need only one since you will not have a huge amount invested for at least a few years), you should pick one that allows small purchases.

If you invest more than 10 per cent of the cost of your self-directed RRSP in international funds, you will be subject to a penalty equal to one per cent per month of the cost of such funds in excess of the 10 per cent limit for as long as the excess remains in your RRSP. The solution is for your RRSP to sell the excess, or you can make an appropriate RRSP contribution to the self-directed plan if you are eligible.

An Attractive Return on Average

Using the step-by-step investing program, you are not going to double the value of your RRSP overnight. But you will earn an attractive return that could result in the value of this year's RRSP contribution doubling every five years. For example, if your RRSP earns income at the average rates of the past 10 years, and you purchased investments in the following proportions:

- 25 per cent money market funds,
- 65 per cent Canadian equity funds from the top performers, and
- 10 per cent international equity fund (a top performer),

you would earn almost 17 per cent annually, which means that it takes a little over four years for your RRSP to double in value. Even if it earns 15 per cent, it takes less than five years to double in value, which is far superior to investing in shorter-term GICs or term deposits at eight per cent and waiting nine or 10 years for your contributions to double in value. In fact, if you contribute regularly for 30 years, you will be four times better off if your RRSP can earn 15 per cent instead of eight per cent on average each year. If it earns 18 per cent, you will be over seven times better off.

You are cautioned to bear in mind that these percentages are based on historical returns. There is no guarantee that investment funds will continue to earn returns of this size in the future. Also remember that there are years when the value of your units in equity funds will decline because the market has performed poorly. However, you are investing for the long term so this should not be too worrisome. In fact, this is the time many investors do their buying because they get better value for their dollars.

Monitoring the Performance of Your RRSP

At least once a year you should check the performance of your investments in your RRSP. The *Financial Post* and *Financial Times* newspapers both publish comparative performance statistics for almost all Canadian mutual funds once a month. If any of your funds is not performing well, sell it and buy one with a good history. Many good funds underperform for one year, sometimes even two, but if one of your funds continues to underperform for any longer, you should probably sell it. You may want to consult with your broker before going through with the sale.

You also may want to keep score each year by calculating the value of your RRSP, say, at the end of the year and comparing this with previous years. Don't forget that, because you are investing primarily in equity funds, in some years the value of your RRSP may actually decline. But in other years it may increase dramatically. In fact, once you have been investing in your RRSP for 15 or 20 years, you might discover that your RRSP earns more investment income in an exceptional year than you did in the workplace.

Because equity funds increase in value much more quickly than the other two investments, it will not be long before 85 or 90 per cent of your RRSP is invested in equity funds. If you want to maintain the balance in your RRSP at 25 per cent money market funds and CSBs, and 75 per cent equity funds, you will have to either continually change the ratio of your contributions or periodically sell some of your equity fund investments. However, bear in mind that most equity funds always have a percentage of their assets invested in interest-bearing securities, sometimes as high as 30 or 40 per cent, and balanced funds could have well over 50 per cent invested in such securities most of the time. Thus, even though 90 per cent of your RRSP may be in equity funds, perhaps only 60 per cent may actually be invested in the stock market at any point in time.

Getting Close to Retirement

As you get closer to retirement you should begin to change your investing technique, unless you have just begun to contribute to an RRSP. Ten years has been arbitrarily chosen as "close to retirement" for several reasons.

In 1989/90, many Canadians have been contributing to their RRSPs for 20 and maybe even 30 years (RRSPs were initiated in 1957) and have sizable amounts accumulated. Most certainly, they want to see continued strong growth in their RRSPs, but more importantly, the need to protect their accumulated capital is now the greatest. There is no point in endangering the retirement income that you can foresee receiving within a few years.

At this point, your *investment horizon* is decreasing rapidly — that is, less and less time remains before you want to begin to use the funds you have invested in your RRSP. And as your investment horizon decreases, the element of risk in many investments tends to increase. As stressed earlier, the risk associated with equity investment funds tends to decrease the longer you hold the investment. In other words, you cannot necessarily expect to obtain the same type of returns you have experienced over the last 15 or 20 years with equity funds, if you invest now but hold them for only a few years.

Another way of looking at your investment horizon is that you now have less time to make up for mistakes. If you buy an equity fund when you are five years from retirement and the market declines over the next three years, you have only two years to make up your losses and just break even.

And, as noted earlier in this chapter, equity fund investments are more risky than money market fund or CSB investments. As well, aggressive and long-term growth equity funds are more risky than balanced funds. Thus, to minimize risk and protect your accumulated RRSP funds, you now begin to focus on low-risk investing — money market funds, CSBs, and balanced equity funds.

If you have been contributing to your RRSP for a number of years in the 25 per cent-75 per cent ratio (25 per cent in money market funds and CSBs, and 75 per cent in equity funds) and have made no adjustments in the composition of your RRSP investments, almost 90 per cent of the value of your RRSP will now consist of equity fund investments. It is now time to begin cutting down this ratio and eliminate some of the risk in your RRSP.

First, all future RRSP contributions should be invested equally in money market funds and Canada Savings Bonds. At this point, you will probably be able to contribute much larger amounts to your RRSP because of reduced family expenses and higher earnings. You should definitely be trying to maximize your allowable contributions at this point, especially if you have the mortgage on your home paid off.

Second, whenever you sell equity fund investments because the fund is not performing up to scratch, all or a portion of the proceeds could be invested in money market funds and CSBs.

Third, you may want to consider replacing some of your investments in aggressive and long-term growth equity funds with investments in balanced funds. This will be especially attractive if the same group operates both types of fund and charges no fees, or perhaps a minimum fee, for transfers between funds. Otherwise, consider the cost of front-end loads. There is no point in incurring a five per cent or six per cent commission if you intend to hold your investment in the balanced fund for only a few years.

Even though you have changed your investing pattern and have switched some of your funds, you will probably still have well over 50 per cent of your RRSP invested in equity funds when you retire 10 years later, and still perhaps even 80 or 90 per cent. If you are planning to convert all your RRSP into a retirement annuity, this can represent an unacceptable level of risk. For instance, a few months before you annuitized your RRSP, the market could go into a tailspin and your retirement income could be 10 per cent or 15 per cent less than you expected. However, under the RRSP retirement income program outlined in Chapter 7, you will not be using the cash invested in equity funds for a number of years, perhaps even 20 years, so risk is minimized.

If you only began contributing to your RRSP when you were 10 or so years away from retiring, you should probably consider maintaining the 75-25 per cent split in investments until close to the time that you mature your RRSP. You will still have the bulk of your money invested in equity funds for a number of years after arranging for a retirement income (see Chapter 7), so you will still be investing for the long term.

CHAPTER FIVE

Make Your RRSP Work Harder For You

BY FOLLOWING THE RRSP contribution and investing program, you will spend less time on your RRSP and should improve the return on your RRSP investments over the long term while keeping risk and worry to a minimum. But this still does not guarantee that your RRSP will do everything you want it to do when you eventually retire. It's a little like trying to build a house with no skilled help. You have all the materials sitting on the lot and you manage to put together some type of structure after a few weeks that more or less resembles the blueprint. But you probably won't want to live in it if the roof leaks, the floors slant, the doors won't close, every room is drafty, and the plumbing, heating, and electricity just don't seem to work properly. If you have gone to the trouble and expense of planning the house to your specifications, you really ought to go all the way and hire skilled persons who can perform the various house-building jobs most effectively. Your house will survive longer than a week or two, and you stand an excellent chance of getting something that you can live in and enjoy for years to come.

Similarly, if you are going to set aside a significant portion of your hard-earned dollars each year for an RRSP contribution, you want the best results possible, which will translate into the best possible retirement income.

Ray and Diane are an average Canadian couple. They both work and make an average family income. Ray contributes $1,000 at the end of each year to his RRSP. He started contributing when he was 30 and plans to retire when he is 62. He has adopted the step-by-step RRSP investing program and, based on historical returns over the last 10 years, expects to earn about 14 per cent on average in his RRSP over these 32 years. If we assume that inflation will average six per cent over this period, Ray's RRSP will grow to about $70,000 by the time he is 62, measured in terms of today's dollars. Using today's rates, this will buy a fully taxable retirement income of about $7,000 a year,* also expressed in today's dollars.

If Ray had not adopted the program, he would be lucky if his RRSP produced a retirement income of $3,000 a year, so he is definitely better off. Still, this potential retirement income is less than 20 per cent of the couple's current total family income. Ray's and Diane's pension plans at work are mediocre at best, so at this rate, they don't expect to be particularly comfortable when they retire.

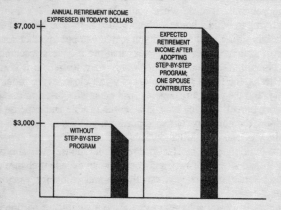

Figure 5.1
Using the Step-by-Step RRSP Investing Program

Ray and Diane have all the materials and tools at their disposal to build up a first-rate RRSP, but currently they are building one with a leaky roof. Let's look at a few techniques everyone, including Ray and Diane, can use to put more muscle into their RRSPs.

---

* It is assumed here and elsewhere that a person in his or her early to mid-sixties can convert $10,000 of RRSP funds into a fully taxable retirement income for life of about $1,000 a year. This income is not indexed to increases in the cost of living, but would continue to be paid to a last surviving spouse. This rate approximates annuity rates (see Chapter 7) in effect in mid-1989. As well, the term "today's dollars" refers to the dollars in the year Ray and Diane started contributing to their RRSPs.

Both Spouses Should Contribute

If you are married, RRSPs should always be looked at from the point of view of both husband and wife. If both of you are working, that is, you both have earned income, both can contribute to your own RRSPs. And definitely, both of you should be contributing. It cannot be said too often — the more you put into your RRSPs, the more you will get out.

As well, if both spouses contribute, you may just pay less tax when you retire, which obviously will increase your standard of living. This is discussed below in the context of spousal RRSPs.

Diane is eligible to contribute over $3,000 a year to her RRSP. By just contributing $500 extra each year and following the same program as Ray, they will be able to collect an RRSP retirement income of about $10,500 (expressed in today's dollars) — a 50 per cent improvement over $7,000.

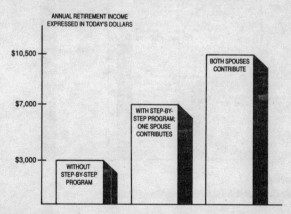

Figure 5.2
Both Spouses Contribute to Their RRSPs

Contribute More by Rearranging Your Finances

A few ways of finding more cash to contribute to your RRSP were outlined in Chapter 2. Every person and every family has at least one way, and probably half a dozen, of freeing up a bit more cash each year to increase the size of their RRSP contributions. Drawing up a budget, specifying the size of your RRSP contribution, and sticking to your plan is the most effective way of raising the necessary cash year after year. Every little bit can make a big difference when it comes time to arrange for a retirement income.

Ray actually has little trouble finding a bit extra. For years, he has been buying Canada Savings Bonds on the payroll savings plan. By opting out of the plan, he has an extra $500 available each year for his RRSP. This brings their total annual contribution up to $2,000. Ray now contributes $1,500 and Diane still puts away $500. Their expected retirement income has risen to about $14,000.

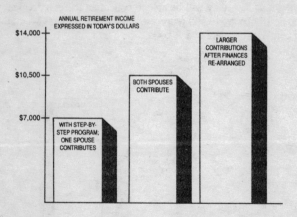

Figure 5.3
Contribute More by Rearranging Your Finances

Contribute Your Tax Refund

One of the first places to look for extra cash is the tax refund that is generated by making your RRSP contribution. In fact, the best thing to do is always think in terms of contributing before-tax cash to your RRSP.

Why not consider a portion of your contribution as a loan that you make to yourself? If you have a few hundred dollars in the bank, borrow from this bank account when you make your RRSP contribution. When you get your tax refund, use the cheque from the government to repay your bank account.

Since their average marginal tax rate is about 33⅓ per cent, Ray and Diane can contribute an extra $1,000 to their RRSPs on top of the $2,000 that they already contribute, if they also contribute their tax refunds. By contributing a total of $3,000, their taxes will be reduced by one-third of this amount, or $1,000. This again increases the size of their potential RRSP retirement income by 50 per cent to about $21,000, expressed in terms of today's dollars.

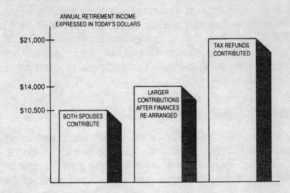

Figure 5.4
Contribute Your Tax Refund

As a bonus for making larger RRSP contributions, Diane will receive an extra $100 from the government in the form of child tax credits. Since they have two children under 18, they are eligible for the child tax credit, which was $565 per child in 1989. However, Diane's credit is reduced by five per cent of family net income beyond a threshold point, which is a little over $24,000 in 1989. By contributing an extra $2,000 to their RRSPs, family net income for tax purposes is reduced by $2,000 because RRSP contributions are deducted from income. This restores $100 of child tax credits (five per cent of $2,000), which Diane will see in the form of a larger tax refund.

Ray and Diane's RRSPs are now in high gear. They can expect a retirement income of $21,000 instead of $3,000, which com-

bined with Government and company pension benefits will
provide a comfortable level of income when they retire. But they
can still do a lot better, and, indeed, they feel they must. For instance, they know that they have to build a degree of inflation
protection into their retirement income if they want to achieve
real security.

Don't underestimate the value of contributing your tax refund.
In reality, Ray and Diane's marginal tax rate is exceptionally low.
The average Canadian family income is between $45,000 and
$50,000 in some provinces. Your marginal tax rate could be *as
high as 43 or 44 per cent*. That means for every dollar you plan
to contribute to an RRSP, you can contribute another 75 or 80
cents that result from the tax saving. No Canadian should will-
ingly consider giving the government close to half of his or her
paycheque when these tax dollars could be put to much better
use in an RRSP.

Contribute at the Beginning of Each Year

The "RRSP season" as far as RRSP issuers are concerned is
January and February for contributions that are made for the
previous year. This is natural since we have until the end of
February to make last year's contribution, and most of us

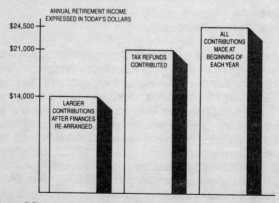

Figure 5.5
Contribute at the Beginning of Each Year

manage to postpone contributing until these two months. A much more effective idea is to treat the RRSP season as applying to the current year, not last year. By making your RRSP contribution at the beginning of each year, rather than waiting to the last minute, you can increase the size of funds accumulated in your plan by 10 or 15 per cent.

If Ray and Diane contribute at the beginning of each year for each of the 32 years they have their RRSPs, they can increase the size of their retirement income to over $24,500 a year.

Monitor Your RRSP Investments

If you follow the RRSP investing program and buy investment funds that perform reasonably well throughout the period of time you have your RRSP, you can safely ignore your investments for long stretches of time and still earn an attractive return. However, periodic monitoring of your investments in light of the general health of the economy can pay off with a one or two percentage point increase in your average return over the long term.

For example, investment funds do not always keep performing the way they have in the past. In fact, it is very unlikely that the three equity funds you originally purchase will all continue to behave well for 20 or 30 years. You should definitely expect to have to replace one or two, or perhaps all of them at some point. As well, in some years as you prepare to make your RRSP contribution, the general consensus of experts may be that the stock market is looking forward to a serious decline. You may be better off in that year using your entire contribution to buy money market funds and CSBs. In the following two or three years, you would buy equity funds exclusively.

Ray and Diane decided to look over their RRSP investments about twice a year and Diane will be responsible for staying attuned to general economic trends since she works for a financial institution. Over the course of their working lives, they expect to increase the average return on their RRSP investments by one percentage point to 15 per cent because of their diligence. They will be amply rewarded for the small amount of effort expended. Their RRSP now will grow fast enough at 15 per cent annually to provide them with an RRSP retirement income of almost $31,000 a year. When this is combined with pension income from their company pensions and Government pension income, they can expect to receive more in terms of today's dollars in the first year they retire than they are earning now.

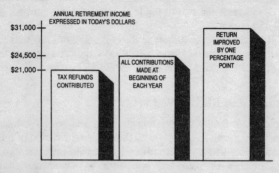

Figure 5.6
Monitor Your RRSP Investments to Improve the Return

Start Contributing as Early in Your Working Life as Possible

It is not easy to convince someone in their twenties that they should begin saving for their retirement. They have a host of other priorities for their hard-earned dollars, all of which seem much more important than contributing to an RRSP. However, beginning your RRSP contribution program at an earlier age can make an astounding difference in the size of your eventual retirement income.

Ray and Diane don't have the option of turning back the clock, but consider the results if they had started contributing to their RRSPs just five years earlier. In this case, their RRSPs would have 37 years to grow instead of just 32. They would accumulate almost 50 per cent more. By starting five years earlier, they would be able to arrange for an RRSP retirement income of about $46,000 expressed in terms of today's dollars. But remember that this income is not indexed. If you want your retirement income to increase each year, you must be prepared to accept smaller payments in the earlier years of retirement. If Ray and Diane arranged to have their income indexed at, say, four per

cent a year, they would still receive about $33,000 in the first
year they are retired. Don't forget that this income is fully taxable.

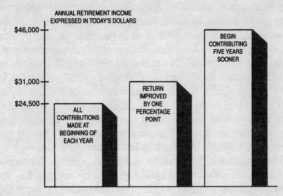

Figure 5.7
Start Contributing as Early in Your Working Life as Possible

Make Spousal RRSP Contributions When Appropriate

You are permitted to contribute to your spouse's RRSP (you must
be married) within your own RRSP contribution limits. This allows your spouse to receive retirement income in the future that
otherwise would have gone to you. Usually, one spouse earns
less income than the other spouse during retirement, often considerably less, and therefore is taxed at a lower rate or sometimes
pays no tax at all. By contributing to a spousal RRSP, retirement
income is shifted from one spouse to the other (from the higher-
income spouse to the lower-income spouse) and this income is
consequently taxed at a lower rate. Any tax savings you can
make means more money in your pocket. This is important
during retirement, especially if you are living primarily on a
fixed income.

Spousal RRSP contributions are easy to arrange. You simply
make the contribution to your spouse's RRSP and indicate to the
issuer or administrator that it is for a spousal contribution. You
will receive the tax receipt and be able to deduct the amount
from your income for tax purposes. Your spouse's contribution

limit is not affected by your spousal contribution. You, on the other hand, must reduce your contribution limit by the amount you contributed to your spouse's RRSP.

If your spouse withdraws funds from any RRSP to which you have made a spousal contribution within three years of the withdrawal, the amount withdrawn is included in your income, not your spouse's, to the extent of all spousal contributions made in the past three years. This rule does not apply if your spouse uses the spousal RRSP funds to arrange an RRSP retirement income, except if such funds are used in two specific cases: if your spouse receives more than the minimum amount from a retirement income fund (RRIF) within the three-year period, or your spouse commutes an RRSP annuity within the same period (see Chapter 7), provided the marriage has not broken down.

After examining their pension plans and potential for receiving Canada Pension Plan and Old Age Security benefits, Ray and Diane determine that Ray will receive considerably more retirement income than Diane. If Ray contributes $1,000 of his total contribution to Diane's RRSP each year as a spousal RRSP contribution, they will have approximately the same income when they are retired. They figure the tax saving could be as high as $2,000 each and every year they are retired.

Contribute a Percentage of Your Income to Your RRSP

Many people make the mistake of contributing a specific amount to their RRSP each year, rather than trying to always contribute a percentage of their income. For example, five years ago you might have been making $20,000 a year and contributed $1,600 to your RRSP, or eight per cent of your income. As a result of promotions and general escalations in wages, your salary has now increased to $32,000. However, you still might be contributing $1,600, which now is only five per cent of your income, but you can probably afford more. Why not continue to contribute at least eight per cent of your income every year, which now amounts to only $2,560? If you belong to a company pension plan, you may be restricted in the percentage of your income that you can contribute to your RRSP.

When Ray and Diane began contributing to their RRSPs, $3,000 was about eight per cent of their total incomes. If they had begun to contribute five years earlier and were to continue contributing eight per cent of their incomes each year for the 37 years, rather than the fixed amount of $3,000, their potential annual RRSP retirement income would jump to over $80,000 expressed in terms of today's dollars (it is assumed that their incomes increase annually by seven per cent, one point above the assumed inflation rate). In fact, by sticking to this plan and arranging an RRSP retirement income indexed at four per cent, Ray and Diane could have well over twice as much in retirement income as they are earning now (today's dollars) in the first year they retire, after taking into account other pension income and Government benefits.

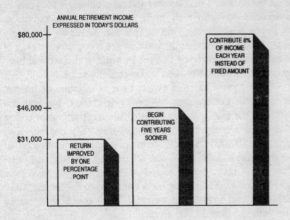

Figure 5.8
Always Contribute a Percentage of Your Income

How Well Will You Do With Your RRSP?

The size of Ray and Diane's retirement income may seem too good to be true. But it's not. Anybody can do exactly what Ray and Diane plan to do. However, retirement income of this size is dependent on a variety of factors, the two most prominent being the requirement that the RRSP earns 15 per cent on average over 37 years and inflation averages six per cent. As well, the couple must maintain their resolve to stick to their plan. Ray and Diane

could be any Canadian couple, but remember that the dollars are
only projections. Rarely does the future work out exactly as you
plan it. Sometimes it may work out better. Maybe Ray and Diane
can contribute more each year and earn 17 per cent. Maybe inflation will average only four per cent.

On the other hand, Ray and Diane may run into financial
problems and be able to contribute only half of what they
originally projected. Perhaps they earn only 13 per cent on their
investments and inflation averages eight per cent. In this case,
they could see their projected RRSP retirement income cut by
two-thirds.

The point is — don't rest on your expectations. Don't put your
RRSP in the back of a desk drawer and forget about it for years or
even decades. And above all, make every effort to contribute as
much as you possibly can. Don't forget that RRSPs are extremely
flexible. If you need the cash, you can get it out of your plan at
almost any time. But if you can get by without it, you will have
that much more available when you eventually retire.

You can't control external events such as inflation or interest
rates or a poor performance by the stock market, but you can
protect yourself from possible disaster. If everything went wrong
for Ray and Diane, they would probably still end up with
$15,000 or $20,000 of RRSP retirement income expressed in
terms of today's dollars. On the other hand, if they had done
nothing about muscling up their RRSPs, they might have only
$2,000 or $3,000. And if they hadn't decided to follow the RRSP
contribution and investment program, they could conceivably
end up with less than $1,000 a year.

CHAPTER SIX

Some Common Questions

E VERYONE HAS questions about their RRSPs and their
personal finances. This chapter answers only a few of
the more common ones. Many questions having to do
specifically with RRSPs are answered throughout the book,
but those of a highly technical nature are not. This book has
been written for average Canadians who want to keep their
RRSPs as simple and productive as possible. If you still have
technical questions after reading the book, you might want to
contact Revenue Canada for some answers, although according to newspaper reports, 100 per cent accuracy is not guaranteed. Tax accountants or tax lawyers will be able to answer all
your questions accurately, but will charge you handsomely.
Make sure the answer you hope to get is worth the bill you
will receive a few weeks later.

Several specific situations that affect many Canadians are
briefly discussed in Appendix C. If your marriage is in danger, or
in the process of breaking down, if you are leaving the country,
or if you are inheriting RRSP funds or estate planning with your
RRSP, and the amounts involved are substantial, you should consider getting professional advice — that is, advice from a tax
professional who is either a chartered accountant or a lawyer.
Other counsellors might be qualified to render quality advice, but
unless you are completely satisfied with their credentials and you
know for a fact that they have given quality advice in the past on
your particular problem, stick to the legal and accounting professionals. They may charge you more, but you will almost invariably get your money's worth.

Should You Use Funds in Your RRSP as a Down Payment on Your First Home?

"Owning your own home is the best investment the average Canadian will make during his or her lifetime." This statement is still as true today as it was in your parents' day and your grandparents'. So the answer to the question is yes — but only if you see no other way of financing the purchase.

A mortgage-free home should be one of the cornerstones of your financial planning for retirement. It is just as important as your RRSP. By owning your own home, you stop paying rent, which always goes up year after year. And owning a mortgage-free home means that your retirement income can be stretched a lot further.

With few exceptions, hardly anybody regrets buying their first home, especially after 10 or 20 years. And it's generally true that unless you have unlimited resources, renting is almost always inferior to owning. In fact, owning a home is the only way most people will be able to live in the type of accommodation they prefer.

How does a home measure up as an investment compared with an RRSP? Bob and Lucy, a couple living in Victoria, have decided to use their RRSP as a down payment on their first home. They have over $24,000 in the RRSP and will get about $20,000 out in cash after paying tax on the withdrawal (see Chapter 2). At the end of 30 years, the house they purchased for $100,000 will be worth about $750,000. The gain on the house is not taxable should they decide to sell. If they had not bought the house, their RRSP would also have grown to almost $750,000 after allowing for taxes. However, since they will pay off their mortgage in 25 years, they will eventually have extra cash to invest that no longer is needed for the mortgage payments. As well, they will have extra cash to invest that is equivalent to the difference between their mortgage payments and the rent they would otherwise be eventually paying if they had not bought the house. For example, in 10 years time, their mortgage payments may still be $700 a month on a $70,000 mortgage, while rents may have increased to $1,100 a month from $600 a month on a similar home. There is every possibility that they would have another $100,000, and maybe up to $400,000, available after taxes with these investments, which makes the house a much better investment than the RRSP.*

If you do use your RRSP as a down payment, try to time the withdrawals from the plan so that the least amount of tax is payable. For example, you may get more back from your RRSP if you withdraw half in December and half in January, so that the withdrawal is taxed in two different years. For an average Canadian, that half withdrawn in January could be taxed at about 26 per cent instead of 40 per cent.

Better still, if your home purchase happens to coincide with a year when one spouse will be out of the work force and have no other source of income, you may be able to eliminate almost all the tax. This spouse would make the larger RRSP contributions to begin with and then would withdraw the funds from the RRSP in the year he or she has no other income. Your tax bill could be reduced by as much as $2,000 or $3,000 dollars, all of which can be put toward the down payment on your new home. This is how Bob and Lucy managed to pay tax of only $4,000 when they withdrew funds from their RRSPs.

Nevertheless, you should definitely try to come up with the down payment for your first home from another source if at all possible. Perhaps you can take out a bigger mortgage, or borrow for a year or two from relatives. Remember what happened to those Chapter 4 RRSP contributions made in the first eight years of a 40-year career. They grew more than all the contributions made in the last 32 years. These "first eight-year" dollars are the same ones that you will use for the down payment on your first home. If you can pay off a second mortgage or the loan from your relatives in a few years, you will end up with both the home and your RRSP still intact, and be all that much better off.

Just because you now own a home does not mean that you should delay your RRSP contributions for a few years or even stop contributing altogether. A fully paid-off home will ease the financial pressures during your retirement years, but steady income from your RRSP will be the source of real comfort and security.

---

* It is assumed that the earnings rate in the RRSP is twice the appreciation rate of the house (14 per cent compared to seven per cent), all taxes at the rate of 40 per cent are paid at the end of 30 years, and the effects of mortgage payments are ignored in the financial calculations because rent would have to be paid in any case.

Should You Use Your RRSP to Save for the Down Payment on Your First Home?

As explained in Chapter 2, RRSPs eliminate tax on the income earned on your net investment if your tax rate does not increase. Your net investment is the amount of, say, employment income that you have left over after paying income tax. This is the same after-tax amount that you can invest and eventually use as a down payment on your first home.

Until the end of 1987, every taxpayer was allowed to earn up to $1,000 of Canadian interest and dividend income tax-free each year. Thus, at current rates, you could invest up to $12,000 or $13,000 in money market funds or Canada Savings Bonds outside an RRSP and still earn the interest tax-free. However, with tax reform, the $1,000 investment income deduction was eliminated.

If you do not own a house and you plan to purchase one, there is no point in paying tax on interest income when you could be earning it tax-free inside an RRSP. There are usually small fees associated with opening an RRSP and withdrawing funds from it or cancelling it, but these will be much less than the tax you will pay on the interest income earned outside the RRSP. One drawback of using an RRSP is the likelihood of your marginal tax rate increasing as your income increases when you are relatively young. Thus, you might end up paying a bit of tax if you contribute to your RRSP when your tax rate is low and withdraw the funds when your tax rate is high.

If you decide to invest in equity funds outside an RRSP in order to save for the purchase of your first home (this is actually too risky an investment for this purpose), any capital gains realized on your investment should be exempt from tax under the lifetime $100,000 capital gains exemption which is available to every taxpayer on almost all forms of capital gains. Thus, you would probably be better off investing outside your RRSP and avoid the special fees.

You should definitely consider saving for the down payment with an RRSP if there is any chance that you can time the withdrawals from the RRSP to coincide with a year when you are not earning other income (see above). The tax saving that results when you cash the RRSP should more than make up for any RRSP fees you might have to pay.

Should You Contribute to Your RRSP or Pay Down Your Mortgage?

The answer is almost simplicity itself. If your mortgage interest rate is higher than your RRSP earnings rate, pay down the mortgage. If the RRSP earnings rate is higher, contribute to your RRSP. The reason why is somewhat more complex, and, of course, nothing is ever truly "simple."

As explained previously, RRSPs eliminate tax on the earnings on your net investment if your tax rate remains the same. Similarly, paying down your mortgage is exactly the same as earning tax-free interest at the mortgage interest rate. Therefore, if both are tax-free investments, choose the one with the better return.

If you have a $10,000 mortgage at 10 per cent, you must pay interest each year of $1,000 (repayment of principal is ignored). Assume that you also have $10,000 invested outside an RRSP that somehow or other earns tax-free interest at the rate of 10 per cent. The $1,000 interest you earn on the investment exactly offsets the mortgage interest you must pay, so you break even. Similarly, if you used the $10,000 to pay off the mortgage you would break even. You would no longer earn the $1,000 of interest but you also would no longer have to pay $1,000 in mortgage interest. Thus, paying off the mortgage is exactly the same as earning tax-free interest income at the mortgage interest rate. You can no longer earn tax-free interest, unless, of course, your income is so low that you are not taxable in any case.

If you follow the RRSP investing program outlined in Chapter 4, you should have a higher earnings rate in your RRSP on average over the long term than the average interest rate on your mortgage over the same period of time. However, if you adopt a very conservative investment stance, paying down your mortgage could indeed be a better investment than the RRSP. For example, mortgage interest rates are usually a point or two higher on average than the interest rate on guaranteed RRSPs such as term deposits or guaranteed investment certificates.

When deciding between your mortgage and your RRSP, there are two other factors to bear in mind. First, if you do not make up your RRSP contribution within the seven-year carry-forward period, there is no other way to catch up for that particular year. Most Canadians will eventually pay off their mortgages. This

will free up large amounts of cash, but by this time you may not
be able to make up for RRSP contributions you did not make because you used the funds to pay down your mortgage instead. In
the long run, you probably would be better off to pay mortgage
interest for a few more years than necessary, and put as much as
possible in your RRSP each year.

Second, if you still have a sizable mortgage when you are less
than 10 years from retiring, you should definitely consider
paying off the mortgage with your RRSP contribution funds. By
this time you will be investing the contributions in money market
funds and Canada Savings Bonds which should be producing a
smaller return than the interest rate on your mortgage. As well,
you should not lose sight of the security afforded by owning a
mortgage-free home during your retirement years.

Should You Contribute to Your RRSP or First Create an Emergency Fund?

As discussed in Chapter 4, there is nothing wrong with treating a
portion of your RRSP as an emergency fund. Investments in money
market funds or CSBs can be cashed quickly and withdrawn easily
from the RRSP. As well, if you do not have to use the funds, you
will have all that much more available for your retirement years.
And as explained above, there is no tax on the earnings on the net
amount invested in your RRSP.

In Chapter 4, it was suggested that you invest the first $5,000
contributed to an RRSP in a money market fund. If you feel more
comfortable, by all means invest the first $10,000 or $15,000.
This is about the same as making a *net investment* of about
$7,000 to $10,000 outside an RRSP.

Should You Earn Capital Gains or Interest in Your RRSP?

Conventional wisdom has it that you should always earn interest
income (income from money market funds and Canada Savings
Bonds) inside your RRSP and realize capital gains, which are
earned on equity funds, outside the RRSP. Up to $100,000 of cap-
ital gains realized during your lifetime outside an RRSP can be
earned tax-free. Retirement income eventually received from

your RRSP is taxed at the same rates as interest income or employment income.

However, as explained earlier, RRSPs eliminate tax on your net investment, so neither interest nor capital gains nor dividends are, in effect, subject to tax when earned inside an RRSP.

If all your investments are inside your RRSP, there is only one rule — maximize your return. And as explained in Chapter 4, this means investing primarily in equity funds on which capital gains will be realized. Why would you want to earn only eight or 10 per cent on interest-bearing investments when your RRSP could be earning 15 per cent or more with equity funds over the long term?

Only if you have maximized your RRSP contributions and you are also investing outside your RRSP would you consider following the conventional rule. In this case, there would be no point in earning taxable interest income outside your RRSP when it could be earned tax-free inside your RRSP. Instead, outside your RRSP you would invest exclusively in securities that produce capital gains, such as equity funds, and increase the size of investments in money market funds and CSBs inside your RRSP.

You can actually buy equity fund investments from your self-directed RRSP to hold outside your RRSP. It is a simple matter for your broker to transfer ownership and there should be no commissions to pay. The cash that you pay to your RRSP then can be used to purchase interest-bearing securities. Note that your self-directed RRSP is like a separate person with whom (or with which) you can transact some types of business, such as buying and selling securities.

Should You Borrow to Make RRSP Contributions?

If you borrow to make an RRSP contribution, the interest paid on the loan is not deductible for tax purposes. This increases the cost of borrowing. For example, if you borrow $1,000 at 12 per cent, you must pay $120 of interest each year. If your marginal tax rate is 40 per cent, you must earn $200 to generate enough income after taxes to pay the non-deductible interest (tax at 40 per cent on $200 is $80 leaving $120 for the interest payment). When interest is deductible from income, the payments are, in effect, made from pre-tax income. Thus, you have to earn only

$120 to pay the deductible interest. Or looked at another way, your cost of borrowing is really only 7.2 per cent instead of 12 per cent, because 40 per cent of your interest expense, or 4.8 per cent, is returned to you in the form of a tax reduction.

Still, you should consider borrowing to make the contribution, if you can repay the loan relatively quickly. During the RRSP season, many RRSP issuers will loan you funds for 12 months at very attractive rates if you invest in one of their RRSPs. If you purchase a short-term security, you could soon transfer the funds to your self-directed plan or to an investment fund.

Borrowing to make a contribution will not be so important beginning in 1990 when the seven-year carry-forward rule takes effect. However, you will still generally be better off borrowing and making the contribution immediately, rather than waiting four or five years to contribute. Human nature being what it is, you just may not get around to making up for the contribution, whereas you will undoubtedly repay the loan.

Rather than borrowing, you might want to consider making monthly contributions to your RRSP in the amount that otherwise would have gone to pay off the loan. There is no significant difference between this and borrowing the funds, except that the consequences of missing a payment to your RRSP are not nearly as severe as missing one to your bank.

Which is Better — an RRSP or a Company Pension Plan?

For many Canadians, the question is academic. Either they have no choice but to join their company pension plan, or their employer does not sponsor one. If they are a member, the only way to supplement pension benefits with the Government's help (that is, receiving tax deductions for contributions) is with an RRSP. The effect of pension reform on company pension plans and RRSPs is discussed briefly in Appendix B.

For a number of other Canadians, the question is like asking which are better — strawberries or raspberries. Just about everybody likes both, but some prefer strawberries over raspberries, and others prefer raspberries over strawberries. If you have a choice of contributing to an RRSP or joining your pension plan, or you can choose between reducing or increasing your pension plan contributions so your benefits are reduced or upgraded, there is no cut-and-dried piece of advice. It all depends on the benefits available from your pension plan, on the amount that becomes available to contribute to your RRSP, and on the rate of return you get in your RRSP.

There is one *very general* rule that you might want to bear in mind. If you have a Cadillac defined benefit registered pension plan — one that provides maximum benefits including indexing of pension benefits — generally, there is little difference between an RRSP and an RPP, assuming that maximum contributions are made to the RRSP and assuming that the investment return in your RRSP is about the same as long term interest rates. However, if you invest primarily in mutual funds and monitor your investments, the rate of return in your RRSP over the long term may consistently be above long-term interest rates.

In real life, hardly any pension plans are indexed, although some provinces may eventually get around to enforcing some type of mandatory indexing, and hardly any average workers belong to Cadillac plans. Thus, an RRSP will probably provide a better pension if equivalent contributions are made.

You should bear in mind, however, that under pension reform, employers must finance *at least half the benefits to be received out of a pension plan.* If you contribute to an RRSP, you must finance the whole contribution yourself. If you opt out of a company plan and are lucky enough to have your wages increased by even part of the amount that your employer would have contributed, there is still no guarantee that you could contribute enough to an RRSP to provide equivalent benefits.

Deciding whether to accept upgrades to your plan is even tougher, assuming you have the choice. It is extremely difficult to measure the value of many of these upgrades, especially in terms of RRSP contributions. Under the new RRSP rules, an upgrade will result in a reduction of your RRSP contribution room. And to make matters even more complex, you might be permitted to use amounts in your RRSP to buy retroactive upgrades in your pension plan. This could be worthwhile, especially if your employer provides matching funding, but it also may not. If the amounts are significant and a number of employees are involved, you might want to consider getting professional advice and share the cost.

It is tempting to simply conclude that most Canadians would probably be better off accepting membership in their company plan and taking any upgrades in the plan, assuming that they have a choice. But, unfortunately, there is no cut-and-dried answer. With pension reform, pension plans are now much more equitable and provide much better benefits. In most cases, it is unlikely that your plan will be so good as to limit your RRSP contributions to only $600 a year. Thus, most workers will have the opportunity to contribute sizable amounts to their RRSPs in order to supplement company pension benefits.

If your company plan does nothing more than provide a pension that is not indexed and is equal to only, say, 30 per cent of your average wages over your entire career, you should definitely plan on making RRSP contributions. Even the Canada Pension Plan and Old Age Security currently pay more than this to a worker making the average wage, and these benefits are indexed.

There has been considerable speculation that with pension reform, many companies will drop their defined benefit plans because they will cost too much to operate. As an alternative, they will encourage employees to use RRSPs. The average Canadian worker should not be dismayed at this prospect. If your employer consequently improves your wages and you contribute regularly to your RRSP according to the program outlined in Chapter 4, you should certainly be no worse off, and in fact could be much better off than you would have been under the pension plan. And you will have the flexibility to arrange the type of retirement income that suits you best.

CHAPTER SEVEN

Retiring With Your RRSP

A S YOU CONTRIBUTE to your RRSP over the years, you have only one goal in mind — to accumulate as much as possible in the RRSP so that you can eventually arrange the largest possible retirement income that best suits your needs during your retirement years. Your total retirement income must satisfy three primary requirements:

- It must cover your expenses each and every year.
- It must provide some form of inflation protection so that your expenses in 10 or 20 years can be covered.
- It must be flexible because circumstances will undoubtedly change over the years.

If you are an average Canadian, you will probably have three, and perhaps four, sources of retirement income.

Government. Assuming certain residency requirements are met, every Canadian begins receiving Old Age Security (OAS) benefits when they turn age 65. And almost all Canadian workers are entitled to Canada Pension Plan (CPP) benefits generally beginning at age 65, although you now can opt to begin receiving them as early as age 60 on a reduced payment basis. Currently, these benefits are indexed according to increases in the Consumer Price Index (that is, the cost of living or inflation). Combined CPP and OAS benefits are designed to replace no more than about 40 per cent of the average Canadian wage. Beginning in 1989, OAS payments received by upper-income retired Canadians are subject to a "taxback." Benefits disappear completely at income levels in the $75,000 to $80,000 range.

Company Pension Plan. Close to half of Canadian employees belong to a company pension plan and will eventually receive pension benefits. Under the recent pension reform, many more Canadians may be joining pension plans. The level of pension benefits you will receive depends on the terms of your plan. If you are retiring in the near future, chances are that your pension benefits will not be indexed.

Private Saving. Most average Canadians will not have significant private savings when they retire. Most, if not all, of their saving will have, or should have, been undertaken through their RRSPs.

RRSPs. The retirement benefits available depend entirely on how much is in the RRSP when you retire and how you arrange your retirement income, the subject of this chapter.

Government and, if available, pension plan income will certainly cover a portion of your retirement expenses, perhaps even the bulk of them initially. But only the Government income is indexed (this could be altered at the whim of the Government of the day), and, generally, neither is at all flexible once you begin receiving payments. Private saving is extremely flexible and inflation protection can be built in depending on how you invest these savings, but few average Canadians have accumulated much in the way of private savings by the time they retire.

Depending on the amount accumulated, RRSPs can supplement these other sources of retirement income, and an RRSP retirement income can be designed to satisfy all three retirement requirements. If you have not accumulated enough in your RRSP, you will have to sacrifice some flexibility and even some inflation protection in order to accomplish the primary goal of meeting your expenses. However, RRSP retirement funds can be arranged to do something pension plan income cannot do — you can continue to invest the bulk of your funds in such a way that more income should become available in later years than would otherwise be the case. This flexible feature of RRSPs is discussed in more detail later in the chapter.

It cannot be stressed too strongly that you should devote considerable time to thinking about and arranging your RRSP retire-

ment income. The time to start is about a year before you plan to
retire. It is possible to paint yourself into a corner you may never
get out of if you rush into things hastily with no preparation or
consideration for the future.

If you have large amounts in your RRSP and these will provide
the bulk of your retirement income, you should consider getting
professional advice, but only after you have done as much
homework as possible. Any advice you get is only as good as the
work you put into it. Above all, an adviser will want to know
your basic income requirements, your spending plans for the
next five or even 10 years, how much you want to continue to
involve yourself with your RRSP retirement income, how concerned you are with leaving a sizable estate to your heirs, and
how much risk you are willing to assume in order to try to improve the size of your retirement income. Reading this chapter
will get you thinking about all these things.

To make the discussion in this chapter more straightforward, it is
usually assumed that funds in your RRSP will be the sole source of
your retirement income. This will almost never be the case because
of the availability of Government pension benefits.

When Can You Mature Your RRSP?

You can mature (the technical term for arranging a retirement income) your RRSP at any time on or before December 31 of the
year you turn age 71. If you have not matured any RRSP by that
date, the full amount accumulated in that plan is included in your
income for tax purposes in the following year. The bulk of these
funds could be taxed at rates as high as 50 per cent depending on
the province in which you live.

You should make sure that the terms of your RRSP allow for
maturity before age 60. Before 1986, you could not mature
RRSPs before turning age 60, so the terms of older plans may
have to be changed, if the issuer has not already done so.

Many taxpayers work until age 71 and others simply don't
need their RRSP funds. But don't make the mistake of leaving the
maturity decision to the last minute. As you will see, the choices
are many and a number of considerations are involved.

Many RRSP plans provide for an automatic maturity if the
administrator is not notified otherwise. The most common type

of retirement income, a life annuity with a 10-year guarantee, will probably be arranged for you. Considering the flexibility now available with RRSPs, this option will probably suit very few people and could leave you severely disadvantaged later in life because the annuity will not be indexed.

You have three maturity options with your RRSP. You may purchase one or more annuities, of which there are a variety of types. You may transfer funds into a registered retirement income fund (RRIF). Or you may simply withdraw funds from your RRSP, in which case they will be included in income for tax purposes in the year of withdrawal. This third option is not at all appealing and should not be considered by anybody. You can choose any of the options and have as many annuities and RRIFs as you like.

Once you turn age 65, the first $1,000 of income in total you receive out of an RRSP annuity and/or an RRIF is eligible for the pension income tax credit. Periodic pension benefits you receive out of a company pension plan are also eligible for this tax credit no matter what your age. The pension income tax credit is calculated as 17 per cent of your eligible pension or RRSP income to a maximum of $1,000, which produces a maximum credit for federal tax purposes of $170. Because federal tax is reduced by the credit, provincial tax will also be reduced. Thus, the total maximum credit will be approximately $260, depending on the province where you live.

The over-age-64 tax credit is $556 beginning in 1989. This credit also reduces federal tax, so the total value of this credit, including provincial tax reductions, will be about $870, depending on the province where you live. This credit is indexed.

If your income is too low to use all or a portion of these two credits, the unused portion may be transferred to your spouse. The transferable portion of your credit generally will be reduced by 17 per cent of your income in excess of $6,000. The calculations for claiming and transferring these credits should be explained in detail in your tax return.

RRSP Life Annuities

There are two basic types of RRSP annuities — life annuities and fixed-term-to-age-90 annuities. Both types come in several varieties. An annuity is simply a contract between you and an annuity issuer. In exchange for a specific amount of cash, in this case cash out of your RRSP, the issuer promises to pay you an income to be received periodically either for life or for a specific number of years. The entire amount received each year from any type of RRSP annuity must be included in income for tax purposes.

A life annuity guarantees to continue payments for as long as you live. If you live to be 101, payments will continue this long. An RRSP life annuity must provide for payments to be made at least once annually. You may arrange for any number of life annuities with RRSP funds.

Life annuities can be issued only by life insurance companies. The cost of a life annuity is based on your life expectancy and current interest rates. The longer you are expected to live according to insurance company statistics, the more an annuity will cost. Similarly, the lower that interest rates are (generally long-term rates), the more the annuity will cost, or looking at the annuity from the point of view of investing a fixed sum, the lower the payments will be. The insurance company invests your lump-sum RRSP amount and makes the payments to you out of the capital and the earnings on it. The less it can expect to make in the future, the less it will be able to pay you.

You can arrange for the payments from a life annuity to be guaranteed to be made, whether or not you die, over a specific period, often 10 or 15 years. If you die before the guarantee period expires, amounts will be available for your heirs. If no guarantee is arranged and you die shortly after receiving the first few payments from the annuity, no amounts are available for heirs. The insurance company keeps everything. Such a guarantee reduces the size of the payments from the annuity (that is, increases its cost).

You can arrange a *joint and last survivor* annuity, with or without a guarantee period. This type of annuity is based on the lives of both you and your spouse, and payments continue until the death of the last surviving spouse. The cost of such an annuity is based jointly on the life expectancies of both spouses. Payments from this type of annuity will be smaller than from a regular life annuity (that is, a joint and last survivor annuity will cost more).

Perhaps the most common type of life annuity arranged with RRSP funds is a joint and last survivor annuity with a 10- or 15-year guarantee. In mid-1989, a joint and last survivor annuity guaranteed 15 years paying about $470 a month could be arranged with $50,000 of RRSP funds by a couple both in their early sixties. This type of annuity pays about 10 per cent less than an ordinary life annuity with a 10-year guarantee. Most annuity brokers will provide quotations at no cost. Check your yellow pages.

Life annuities may have a variety of other features. For example, you may be able to arrange a life annuity that can be commuted at any time. This simply means that you can cancel it and receive a lump-sum from the insurance company. This feature will either increase the cost of the annuity and/or you will pay a hefty fee if you do happen to commute the annuity. If the commuted amount is not transferred directly to another RRSP annuity or to an RRIF, it must be included in income for tax purposes in the year it is received.

You can arrange to purchase a life annuity that is indexed in some fashion. It may be indexed by a fixed amount (the maximum per year is currently four per cent). Or you can purchase an annuity with payments that increase each year according to increases in the value of a pool of assets or according to current interest rate levels. You can even buy an annuity with payments that will increase according to increases in the Consumer Price Index (inflation). All these features increase the cost of the annuity considerably. For example, this last type of annuity (fully indexed) could cost as much as 50 per cent more than a regular annuity that provides for the same payment in the first year.

RRSP Fixed-Term Annuities

Your RRSP can also be used to acquire a fixed-term annuity (also called a term certain annuity). This type of annuity guarantees payments for the duration of the annuity which is for a specific number of years (the term of the annuity). These annuities may be purchased from life insurance companies as well as trust companies. Any number may be purchased with RRSP amounts. The cost of fixed-term annuities depends on the term and on current interest rates.

The term of a fixed-term RRSP annuity is determined by subtracting your age when you buy the annuity from 90. Thus, if you are 62, you can buy a 28-year fixed-term annuity. The term of the annuity can also be based on your spouse's age if he or she is younger than you. Payments must be made from the annuity at least once annually.

Fixed-term annuities can be indexed, and annuities that can be commuted should be available. In mid-1989, a 28-year fixed-term annuity can be purchased for a couple both 62 years of age at about the same cost as a joint and last survivor life annuity with a 15-year guarantee.

Registered Retirement Income Funds (RRIFs)

An RRIF is almost the same as an RRSP, except instead of making contributions to it each year, you receive income from the RRIF. This income is generated from RRSP funds that you have transferred to the RRIF plus earnings on these funds. Income continues to be earned in the RRIF on a tax-free basis. You may have any number of RRIFs you wish. In each year that you own an RRIF, a minimum amount must be received from each RRIF, but there is no maximum. Thus, if you need extra funds one year for medical reasons or perhaps an extended vacation, sufficient funds can be withdrawn from the RRIF.

RRIFs are by far the most flexible of the RRSP retirement income options. Depending on the amount in the RRIF and the earnings generated, practically any income arrangement can be made.

An RRIF is established by transferring funds or investments from your RRSP to the RRIF. In fact, your RRSP can effectively be registered as an RRIF if you are satisfied with your current administrator. Allowable RRIF investments are almost identical to those eligible for an RRSP. Depository RRIFs can be invested in savings accounts and in term deposit or GIC type of investments, except the investment must be structured to allow for at least annual payments of the required minimum amount. You can also invest in mutual funds that are registered as an RRIF, or you can open a self-directed RRIF that can invest in the same wide variety of investments in which RRSPs can invest, except for annuities.

If you have been following the step-by-step RRSP program and you currently have a self-directed RRSP, you would simply have the RRSP converted into an RRIF at the appropriate time.

There should be no commissions involved when your investments are switched from your RRSP to your RRIF, since the transaction is not a sale but rather a simple transfer of ownership (from RRSP trust to RRIF trust). However, there may be a few unavoidable fees involved both with your mutual fund investments and with the RRIF itself.

As part of the RRIF contract, the administrator of the plan will arrange for you to receive payments from the RRIF. These must begin by the end of the year following the year you establish the RRIF and they must be made at least annually. Most taxpayers will opt for more frequent payments. The total amount of all payments from all RRIFs must be included in income for tax purposes in the year received.

You may transfer amounts from one RRIF directly to another on a tax-free basis. And at any time, you may purchase an RRSP annuity with RRIF amounts with no immediate tax consequences, if the payment is made directly from the RRIF.

RRIFs are designed to be held until you are 90 years old. You also may opt for the term of the RRIF to be based on your spouse's age if he or she is younger than you. The minimum payment that must be made from each RRIF each year, beginning in the year after the year that you establish the RRIF, is based on your age, or your spouse's age, at the beginning of the particular year and the value of your RRIF at the beginning of that year. The actual formula is:

$$\frac{1}{\text{90 minus your age, or spouse's age, at beginning of the year}} \times \frac{\text{Value of RRIF at beginning of the year}}{}$$

Thus, if you are 65 years of age at the beginning of a year and you have \$100,000 in your RRIF at that time, at least \$4,000 must be received from the RRIF, calculated as:

$$\frac{1}{90 - 65} \times \$100,000 = \frac{1}{25} \times \$100,000 = \$4,000$$

If this formula is followed through to the point where you are age 89 at the beginning of the year, the entire amount of the RRIF will finally be exhausted in that year. By law, all amounts must be paid out of the RRIF in the year you turn age 90. No minimum amount need be paid from the RRIF in the year it is established.

Figure 7.1 shows how the minimum payment increases each year if the above RRIF earns 12 per cent annually and the payment is made at the end of each year.

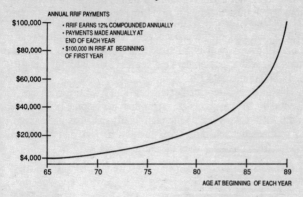

Figure 7.1
Minimum Payment Schedule From RRIF Over 25 Years

Most Canadians will opt to receive quite a bit more than the minimum amount in most if not all years, and most will want the payments to be indexed. The following example shows how an RRIF works in practice. Jack and Maria, a Toronto couple, opened up an RRIF towards the end of December. On January 1 of the following year, there was $100,000 in their RRIF. They based the payment schedule on Maria's age, which was 65 on that January 1. To simplify the numbers, it is assumed that the payments are made at the end of each year.

Before opening up the RRIF, Jack and Maria sat down with their family budget and estimated that they would need about $9,500 from the RRIF in the first year. Based on the experience they had with their RRSPs, they figured that they should be able to earn at least 12 per cent compounded annually in the RRIF. By the end of the first year, their RRIF has earned $12,000 (12 per cent of $100,000), so there is a total of $112,000 in the RRIF. At that point, $9,500 is paid out, leaving $102,500 ($112,000 minus $9,500).

When figuring out their income needs, Jack and Maria also decided that they wanted their RRIF payments to be indexed to some extent. Their RRIF administrator calculates that the RRIF will be exhausted when Maria turns age 90 if payments are indexed at four per cent and if the RRIF continues to earn 12 per cent. In the second year, the RRIF earns $12,300 (12 per cent of $102,500), so there is $114,800 ($102,500 plus $12,300) in the RRIF at the end of the second year. The payment that year is about $9,870, which is $370 or four per cent higher than the previous year's payment. This leaves $104,930 in the RRIF ($114,800 minus $9,870).

This process is repeated each year until Maria reaches age 90. Eventually, the payments are larger than the income being earned in the RRIF each year, so the plan finally exhausts itself. Figure 7.2 outlines the schedule of payments that Jack and Maria will receive from this RRIF over the entire 25 years.

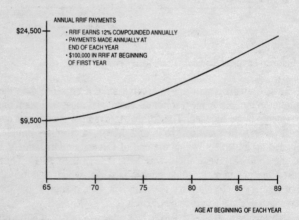

ANNUAL RRIF PAYMENTS

• RRIF EARNS 12% COMPOUNDED ANNUALLY
• PAYMENTS MADE ANNUALLY AT END OF EACH YEAR
• $100,000 IN RRIF AT BEGINNING OF FIRST YEAR

AGE AT BEGINNING OF EACH YEAR

Figure 7.2
RRIF Payments Indexed at Four Per Cent Over 25 Years

Your RRSP Retirement Program

Under the RRSP retirement program, RRIFs, not annuities, are used to generate your retirement income. There are three main reasons why:

1. RRIFs are much more flexible than annuities. You can arrange to receive your income in practically any manner, and change it when circumstances dictate. If you think you will live past age 90 when you must give up your RRIF, you can even buy an RRSP life annuity with RRIF funds.

2. With an RRIF, you should be able to arrange a much better retirement income than with an annuity, and take on very little additional risk — perhaps no additional risk at all (see #3). In fact, one of the objectives of the retirement program is to provide you with exactly the same income in the first year of retirement that an annuity would provide, but have this income indexed at least to age 90.

3. While some of the investments in an RRIF may be considered somewhat risky, for instance, investment funds, an RRIF itself may actually be less risky than buying an annuity. The size of the payments of any annuity you buy is based on current long-term interest rates. What happens if interest rates are currently nine per cent, but increase to 14 per cent after you have committed yourself to the annuity? This probably indicates that inflation is running at 10 per cent or 12 per cent a year, which means the cost of living could be doubling every six or seven years. Anybody with a level payment annuity (one whose payments are not indexed) would soon be in serious trouble. But if you have an RRIF that has invested in a variety of securities, income over the long term should increase as the inflation rate increases. This means that you can receive larger payments from the RRIF to keep up with increases in the cost of living. If inflation declines, you will be no worse off with the RRIF if a portion is invested in equity funds, since these normally perform well when inflation is low and the economy is healthy. It is possible that you could be fortunate enough to lock in a life annuity when interest rates are at their peak. However, insurance companies are notoriously conservative when setting annuity rates.

There are two small drawbacks to an RRIF that you should be aware of. First, the return on your investments and therefore the size of your retirement income is not guaranteed the way it is with an annuity. If this is a concern reread #3 above. By no stretch of the imagination do guaranteed annuity payments automatically eliminate all risk. Second, you may be tempted to withdraw too much money from your RRIF early on in your retirement which will reduce the size of your income in future years. This is impossible with an annuity, unless you opt to commute it. Your only defence against this second drawback is your own will power.

Self-Directed RRIFs

It is not absolutely necessary to have a self-directed RRIF (see below), but it usually won't hurt. Self-directed RRIFs operate exactly like self-directed RRSPs (see Chapter 4), except that the administrator must ensure that you receive at least the required minimum amount of income each year. You can hold almost all the same investments in a self-directed RRIF, including mutual funds and Canada Savings Bonds.

Are self-directed RRIFs too risky for retired persons? It is often argued that retired persons usually don't have the inclination to take care of their investments in a self-directed RRIF, especially as they get on in years. And it is argued that retired persons should not be entertaining the "risk" associated with self-directed RRIFs.

The risk question was discussed above. RRIFs, and especially self-directed RRIFs, just may be less risky than annuities over the long term. And to answer the first objection, arrangements can be made to have the self-directed RRIF virtually run itself.

Under the retirement program outlined in this chapter, your self-directed RRIF invests in three or maybe four different investments — equity funds, money market funds, CSBs, and income funds (a new investment). As with the RRSP, these should require little maintenance, and many people will hold onto the same funds for almost as long as they have their RRIF. You should definitely open your self-directed RRIF with a full service broker. You can leave standing instructions with the broker and a power of attorney with your lawyer, both of which should ensure that your RRIF takes care of itself if you lose interest or become incapacitated for any reason.

As well, a self-directed RRIF, just like a self-directed RRSP, allows you to invest up to 10 per cent of the cost of the RRIF in foreign investment funds. You can transfer between investments much more easily with a self-directed RRIF, your record keeping and reporting will be simplified, and most importantly, your instructions go to only one person — your broker — rather than a variety of funds. You might pay additional fees for the service, but in the long run it should be worth the extra cost.

Your investment in most mutual funds can be structured as an RRIF. Thus, if you do not want a self-directed RRIF, you could buy into, say, four or five different funds and instruct each one to distribute the appropriate amount to you periodically. However, you are now dealing with four or five administrators and you may lose some flexibility. For example, you may be able to leave a standing order with your broker to increase your annual payments by four per cent each year unless you notify him or her otherwise. With some funds, you may have to notify them each year to increase the payments. It also may be more difficult to arrange lump-sum payments, whereas with a self-directed RRIF you simply instruct your broker to provide the payment.

Transfers to Your RRIF

As noted above, the administrator of your self-directed RRIF should be a full service broker. If you are happy with the broker you are using for your RRSP, simply instruct him or her to transfer your investments to an RRIF. Again, there will be a form to fill out, similar to the RRSP form. It may take a few weeks or perhaps even a month or two to get all the preliminaries over with so you can begin receiving payments, so be sure to start the transfer process early enough.

It is assumed throughout this chapter that, like Jack and Maria, you are transferring $100,000 from your RRSP to your RRIF and you are 65 years old at the beginning of the year you receive your first payment. To some of you, this may seem like a lot, but bear in mind that if you contribute $3,000 at the beginning of each year to your RRSP for 12 years and earn 15 per cent, you will accumulate over $100,000 at the end of 12 years. Many Canadians now have over $100,000 in their RRSPs, and almost everybody in their thirties or forties should have no trouble accumulating well in excess of $100,000 by the time they retire. Remember that $100,000 in 20 years will not have the same purchasing power as $100,000 today.

It is also assumed that you want to begin receiving a substantial retirement income from the RRIF shortly after you retire. If you do not need at least the minimum payment that must be made from the RRIF each year, there is no point in opening one the day you retire. It is just as easy to withdraw any amounts needed from your RRSP and avoid the various RRIF fees. You can also convert only part of your RRSP to an RRIF, if you desire, and later mature the remaining portion.

Unused Contribution Room

In not too many years, many persons will have unused RRSP contribution room available when they retire (see Chapter 3). They can still make tax deductible contributions to an RRSP even though they are no longer earning employment or self-employed income. There is no point in receiving RRIF amounts and then contributing them to an RRSP. One simply cancels out the other. You are better off to leave the RRSP contribution room alone in case you receive some type of taxable income before you turn age 72 which is in excess of your income needs in the particular year.

For example, suppose that you are receiving Government pension benefits, pension plan benefits and amounts from your RRIF, and you unexpectedly receive $20,000 which is taxable. You can reduce your RRIF payments to the minimum, but you still have more than enough to live on for that year. In this case, you could contribute the excess income to an RRSP up to your contribution room limit. This will reduce your taxes and any income earned on that excess in the future will not be taxed while in your RRSP. Subsequently, you will transfer the RRSP amount to your RRIF. As a result, you will eventually be able to receive extra income from the RRIF because more money will be in it.

If you have RRSP contribution room available and savings outside an RRSP that are producing taxable income, you should give serious consideration to contributing them to an RRSP and then transferring the amount to an RRIF. You will reduce your taxes in that year, eliminate tax on the investment income earned on your savings, and you can withdraw the amounts at any time from your RRIF. Of course, tax will be payable on the withdrawal, but as demonstrated in Chapter 2, there is no tax on the earnings on your net investment in an RRSP.

Determining the Size of Your RRIF Income

Since the income you will receive from your RRIF is more
flexible than other sources of income, it makes sense to adjust it
according to your needs. If you have not yet been informed of
your OAS and CPP benefits, the Federal Department of Health
and Welfare might be able to estimate them for you. If you are
employed or will be receiving a company pension, you should be
able to easily find out the size of your pension benefits. And if
you have savings outside an RRSP, you should be able to estimate the size of the income that will be generated.

Once you know how much income you will be receiving, you
then need to determine your income needs and any resulting tax
liability. A recent tax return will come in handy to make the
proper calculations.

Jack and Maria went through the calculations outlined below.
They figured that they would be receiving $11,000 in OAS and
CPP benefits, and another $6,500 in company pension plan
benefits in the year they retired. They also determined that they
would need about $25,000 after taxes. After doing some simple
calculations using a tax return, they estimated that they would
have to receive about $27,000 before taxes. Tax on this amount
would be less than $2,000, which produces $25,000 ($27,000
minus $2,000). This means that the RRIF had to produce about
$9,500 ($27,000 minus total OAS, CPP, and pension of $17,500)
in the first year.

However, Jack and Maria wanted their income to be indexed
to some extent. Using current figures, they estimated that three or
four per cent indexing a year should be adequate. Their Government benefits are fully indexed at the moment, but their pension
plan benefits are not. Therefore, they estimated that they had to
index their RRIF payments by at least four per cent a year to
produce an overall indexing of about three per cent. With the
help of their broker who administers the RRIF, they determined
that the RRIF must generate an annual income of about 12 per
cent compounded annually to provide an RRIF income indexed at
four per cent with a first annual payment of about $9,500. They
had been averaging about 14 or 15 per cent in their RRSPs, so
they figured that by investing in less risky investments with their
RRIF, they should have little trouble averaging 12 per cent.

In mid-1989, $100,000 would buy a joint and last survivor life annuity with a 15-year guarantee term for a couple both 65 years old, paying a little over $10,000 a year, but this annuity would not be indexed. In other words, when you are 85, the life annuity would still pay about $10,000 a year. However, by the same date, the indexed RRIF would be paying over $20,000 a year.

If you decide that the first payment from your RRIF must be, say, $11,000 a year instead of $9,500, you will either have to take more risk so that the RRIF might earn more over the long term, or you can cut down on the indexing. For example, in this situation, the RRIF would have to earn about 14 per cent a year to generate an initial payment of $11,000 still indexed at four per cent. Or you could reduce the indexing to about two per cent and still assume that the RRIF will earn 12 per cent a year.

Will You Need More Income in the Early Years of Retirement?

Retired persons tend to spend more in the few years immediately after retiring than in succeeding years. It's now time to do all the things that you have planned. And chances are that you are in better physical shape to do them now than you will be in 10 or 15 years. Almost all these activities will cost money and to some extent will affect the size of your retirement income in later years.

If you have other savings, this is the easiest and most logical place to go for the extra cash you need for that once-in-a-lifetime vacation or a winter home in a more hospitable climate. If you do not have enough savings, the cash will have to come out of your RRSP or RRIF. It will generally be more convenient to transfer all your RRSP investments to your RRIF and make the special withdrawals from the RRIF as you need them. There is little point in leaving your self-directed RRSP intact and needlessly paying the annual administration fee. Depending on the extra amounts that you withdraw, you may have to recalculate how much you will be able to receive from the RRIF given a specific earnings rate.

For example, suppose that you need about $13,000 in each of the first four years from your RRIF instead of the $9,500 indexed at four per cent. In this case, you would have to accept a reduced payment schedule in the following 21 years. Assuming the RRIF continues to earn 12 per cent compounded annually and payments are indexed at four per cent beginning in the fifth year, the payment in that year would be reduced to about $9,650 from $11,100.

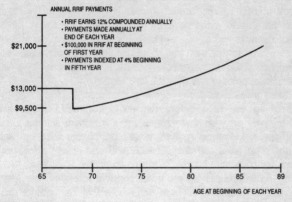

Figure 7.3
Larger RRIF Payments First Four Years

Pre-Arranged RRIF Withdrawals

It is an easy matter to provide instructions so that specific amounts are received from your RRIF. Most investment funds allow you to set up a program of withdrawing specific amounts from the fund either monthly, quarterly, semi-annually, or annually. As well, you and the administrator of your self-directed RRIF will work out a schedule of payments from the plan.

For example, assume that your RRIF is invested in five different funds and you have $10,000 in CSBs. You and your broker will decide on the amount to withdraw from each fund and how often you will receive payments (your broker will provide instructions to the fund). As well, the two of you will decide how much to withdraw from the CSBs each year. It is at this point that you should listen to the advice of your broker. If he or she expects the stock market to perform well in the year, it may be advisable to cut down on the payments from your equity funds and increase them from other investments. You will still receive the same amount during the year, but it will come predominantly from the poorer performing investments. If interest rates are on the rise, you may be looking forward to a year or two of poor performance from your income fund investments (see below). Therefore, you could increase the amount paid from these. If the stock market has performed spectacularly for several years, it may be time to withdraw extra money from your equity funds since the next year or two will probably produce smaller gains or even a loss. In this way, you should be able to improve the performance of the investments in your RRIF, perhaps even by a full percentage point or two over the long term.

Most investment funds require a minimum amount to be invested in the fund before they will institute a systematic withdrawal program, and they require a minimum amount to be withdrawn each time. As well, most funds charge a fee for each withdrawal. Your self-directed RRIF will also charge a fee, perhaps for each withdrawal. To cut down on the amount of RRIF fees you will be paying, you might consider receiving your RRIF payments quarterly, or even semi-annually. You would then withdraw the money from your savings account as you need it. However, remember that the interest you earn on the savings account will be taxed. Assuming that bank account interest rates stay in the five per cent range, not that much interest will be earned, and the tax payable may be less than the RRIF fees that you would otherwise pay. Try to do the appropriate calculations before you commit yourself to quarterly or semi-annual RRIF payments.

If you have a self-directed RRIF, your broker will arrange for the RRIF payments to be increased each year according to the percentage you desire. You could simply instruct your broker to increase the payments by, say, four per cent each year unless you instruct him or her differently. You can dictate the size of the payments to come from each investment each year, or you can leave this up to the discretion of your broker. The emphasis in this book has been on *letting qualified professionals make investment decisions for you*. This becomes even more important during retirement. Deciding how much to receive from each investment is an investment decision, since the earnings in your RRIF, and consequently the size of your RRIF payments, both now and in the future will be affected by the choices made.

Investing With Your RRIF

When you transfer the investments in your self-directed RRSP to your self-directed RRIF, there is every possibility that almost 90 per cent will consist of equity fund investments, even though you have bought nothing but money market funds and CSBs the past 10 years. It is simply a case of equity funds outperforming money market funds and Canada Savings Bonds by a wide margin on average over the long term. Some of you may have less in equity funds, because you were following a program of converting some of your investments to money market funds or CSBs. In any case, the percentage should start coming down once these investments are in your RRIF.

If you transfer $100,000 into your RRIF in your early sixties and index your RRIF income at about four per cent a year, about $35,000 of the funds transferred into the RRIF plus earnings on the $35,000 will be used to finance payments during the first five years of your retirement. About $25,000 of the amount transferred plus earnings will be used for payments in the next five years, and the remaining $40,000 plus earnings will be used for payments in the remaining years until you are age 90. This means that up to $60,000 or 60 per cent of the funds transferred plus the income earned on these funds will be used during the first 10 years of your retirement. If long-term investments are considered to be those held for more than 10 years or so, a great deal more than 10 per cent of your RRIF should be invested for the shorter term. As well, there should be less risk associated with these investments than with the 40 per cent that will not be used for at least 10 years.

The more conservative your RRIF investments, the less likely it is that your RRIF will suffer a decline in value and the more likely it is that you can stick to your payment schedule. However, as explained above, "eliminating risk" by buying an annuity can actually be more risky than relying on an RRIF. Therefore, your goal with the RRIF is *to eliminate large fluctuations in value while maintaining the earnings at a level that will support your indexed payments.*

You are investing a sizable portion of your RRIF for the long term, but you are also withdrawing amounts periodically, so you do not benefit from the effects of compounding the way you did with your RRSP. If you withdraw $14,000 from your RRIF one year and it also declines in value by $14,000, the amount of earnings in future years that will be used to finance future payments will be seriously impaired.

Some investment advisers use the rule of thumb that the amount you should have invested in conservative, interest-bearing securities be at least equal to your age expressed as a percentage. Thus, if you are 65, you should have 65 per cent of your RRIF invested in money market funds, CSBs, etc. and only 35 per cent in equity funds. This conservative approach might have been okay 20 or 30 years ago when many people didn't expect to reach age 70 and the inflation rate seldom went above two or three per cent. But if you expect to be alive and kicking well past age 90, you need the higher earnings potential of equity funds to continue to provide you with an adequate income.

By the end of the fifth year after you have opened your RRIF, you might consider having your RRIF invested in the following proportions:

- 50 to 60 per cent in equity funds
- 25 per cent in money market funds and Canada Savings Bonds
- 15 to 25 per cent in income funds.

If your RRIF is self-directed, you should still have 10 per cent of the cost of the RRIF invested in a fund that invests in foreign stocks. If the one you were using with your RRSP has been performing well, keep it. You may want to tilt your remaining equity fund investments towards balanced funds rather than aggressive or long-term growth funds. Remember that a sizable portion of the investments made by your equity funds could be in interest-bearing securities.

It is not as important to invest in Canada Savings Bonds with your RRIF since you will be using income funds. Canada Savings Bonds offer some protection during the year if interest rates decline. This same protection is offered with income funds.

An income investment fund is no different from an equity fund or a money market fund, except that most if not all its investments are made in interest-bearing investments. The ones that invest primarily in bonds and/or mortgages are the ones you want. Historically, the larger income funds have performed about one to one-and-a-half percentage points better than money market funds on average over the past 10 years, but several of the best performing income funds have averaged three percentage points better. Income funds, and particularly bond funds, tend to perform extremely well when interest rates are declining, but do not do very well when interest rates are rising rapidly.

Few income funds have a front-end load, but several of those that do have performed very well. If you are paying, say, a five per cent commission, the fund must outperform other funds with no commission by at least half a percentage point over at least 10 years in order for you to be as well off.

By the end of the tenth year, after you have established your RRIF and certainly by the time you are 75, you should consider having no more than about 40 per cent of your RRIF invested in equity funds, and about 30 per cent in money market funds or CSBs, and 30 per cent in income funds. These proportions can swing up or down to some extent depending on your tolerance to risk, but remember that the idea is for your RRIF to perform well enough to provide you with an adequate indexed income. If it provides more than you can possibly use, you can reduce the risk. If it is not providing enough, you may have to increase the risk slightly (that is, invest a larger proportion in equity funds), but you should also consider cutting down on your expenses if possible so that the RRIF continues to provide a reasonable income to at least age 90.

If you were earning 15 per cent or more on average with your RRSP, you should have no trouble earning at least 12 or 13 per cent with your RRIF. In fact, using historical 10-year average earnings rates at mid-1989, the following investments in an RRIF would have produced an annual earnings rate of over 13.5 per cent:

- 10 per cent in a foreign equity fund earning 20 per cent
- 25 per cent in a long-term growth equity fund earning 16 per cent
- 25 per cent in a balanced fund earning 14 per cent
- 25 per cent in a money market fund earning 10 per cent
- 15 per cent in an income fund earning 11 per cent.

Converting Investments

Over the first 10 or so years of owning your RRIF, you will probably be converting many of your equity fund investments into money market funds and income funds. There are two cardinal rules you should observe when selling and buying investments in the funds:

1. Don't sell your equity funds when the stock market is depressed. At this point the value of your funds has probably declined but it is also at this time that the investment professionals are beginning to load up on stocks because prices are down. You should follow their lead and hold onto your equity funds. The market will recover and the value of your funds should increase rapidly.

2. Don't buy income funds when interest rates are rising. Income funds, particularly bond funds, perform poorly as interest rates rise. You are much better off with money market funds at this point.

So how do you know when the market has hit bottom or interest rates are going to rise significantly? This is when the broker who should be administering your self-directed RRIF again comes in handy. He or she will be aware of market trends and expectations. Let this professional make these investment decisions for you. The overall performance of your RRIF, and as a consequence the size of your retirement income, will get a shot in the arm.

What if You Live Past Age 90?

You cannot have an RRIF past the age of 90, and, in fact, the minimum payout formula is designed to exhaust all funds in the RRIF in the year you reach 90. So how do you put food on the table if you live to be 101?

The income needs of most people decline as they get older. They have made all their major purchases, done most of their major travelling, and have settled into a lifestyle with predictable spending patterns. In fact, after you have been retired for 10 or

15 years, you might discover that your RRIF and other sources of retirement income are providing more than you need, if, of course, they were providing adequately over the first 10 or 15 years.

The first thing to do when this happens is to reduce the size of your RRIF payments. This will act to increase the amount accumulating in your RRIF. Remember that at any point, you may buy a life annuity with RRIF funds and there will be no immediate tax consequences. This life annuity could serve to replace the income that no longer is being received from your RRIF.

For example, suppose that at age 75, you reduce your RRIF payments by about $3,000 a year. These reduced payments still escalate at four per cent a year of course. By the time you reach your late eighties, you could have enough extra in your RRIF to buy a life annuity paying more than what you were receiving from your RRIF. You may even be able to index it and receive somewhat less, but still enough to live on comfortably.

Of course, this plan depends completely on your income needs being reduced at some point in your seventies. If you still need the income and you need it indexed, it will run out by the time you reach age 90. The only options open to you are to cut down the size of the income, cut down the indexing, take more risk in your RRIF so more hopefully is earned by the investments, or buy a life annuity now. However, this last option does you no good, since you will be lucky to even replace your existing income and the annuity won't be indexed. Unfortunately, there are no other solutions. That is why you want to accumulate as much as possible in your RRSP during your working years so you can avoid unpleasant decisions like this.

In case you become incapacitated for any reason, you should consider leaving an appropriate power of attorney with your lawyer to ensure that any excess funds in your RRIF are converted to a life annuity before your RRIF expires, if it looks like you will live past age 90. You should also leave similar written instructions with your broker. Bear in mind that these comments and all others in this chapter apply to both you and your spouse.

High Interest Rates and Life Annuities

Retired persons, or those about to retire, are occasionally advised to purchase life annuities if interest rates are extremely high. Of course, this means that you will receive larger payments from the annuity than if it is purchased when interest rates are lower. There are problems with this plan of action. First, it is impossible to guarantee that interest rates have peaked at some point and won't go higher, either next week or next year. Second, insurance companies have been successful over the centuries because they are conservative. Interest rates may be at a point where you can buy a GIC for 20 per cent, but the rates that the insurance companies use for purposes of determining payments on life annuities may be as low as 11 per cent or 12 per cent. You can do better than this over the long term with an RRIF, especially if interest rates are at 20 per cent for a period of time.

APPENDIX A

RRSP and RRIF Investments

Investment Funds

The October 1987 stock market crash put a cloud over mutual fund sales, particularly equity funds (those that invest primarily in stocks). Just about everyone expected the market to drop, but nobody thought it would be that precipitous. And human nature being what it is, many thought that they would escape unscathed. The market recovery has been strong, and, if it continues, the gains over the past few years could be close to the average of the last ten or fifteen years. As well, signs of a recession are fading, and, even though interest rates have gone up a bit, they are not expected to get up into the 20 per cent range that we saw in 1981/82.

So, will investment funds continue to perform as they have? The answer is yes and no. Over the short term, who knows? Some say the October crash was a harbinger of further major declines. And others see the crash as the shortest bear market in history, a blip in the numbers that we will laugh about in the near future. But bear in mind that the general movement of the stock market over the long term has been up — and there is no reason to think this will change. Thus, equity funds should continue to move upward — *over the long term*.

The direction that interest rates will take over the next year or two is anybody's guess. If interest rates remain stable or increase somewhat, income funds (those that invest in interest-bearing securities) will not perform particularly well, especially when compared with their performance over the last six years (income funds do best when interest rates are declining). Nevertheless, income funds should, *over the long term*, produce a better return than you will be able to get from most other interest-bearing investments.

But Canadians also invest in mutual funds for other reasons. By investing in several funds, they participate in a wide variety of investments, something they could not do personally because their resources are limited. With the funds, they are buying into a balanced portfolio of securities. More importantly, though, they recognize the value of professional investment advice and are willing to let these experts (the managers of the funds) invest on their behalf.

And more and more Canadians are turning to mutual funds to simplify their financial affairs. Once they have decided on a fund, all investment decisions are made for them by the professionals managing the fund. They don't have to be aware of the hundreds of different investments on the market, or worry about buying low and selling high, or track the daily performance of the stock market and many different investments. They simply have to monitor the performance of the few funds they have purchased, and this only need be done periodically, even once a year if they are investing for the *long term*.

The two words "long term" have come up over and over again in the book. It cannot be stressed too strongly that most RRSP and RRIF investing is for the long term. Only Canada Savings Bonds and money market investment funds are considered to be short-term investments. Long term is considered to be at least seven or eight and almost always more than 10 years. If you invest in equity or income funds for any less time, you are speculating with your retirement income which means the chances for disappointment increase dramatically. If you have extra funds outside your RRSP, by all means take a chance with them if you are so inclined. If you lose everything, you will still be able to put food on the table, pay your mortgage, and look forward to a comfortable retirement.

What Are Mutual Funds?

A mutual fund, or investment fund, is a pool of cash received from investors that is invested by an expert, or group of experts. In theory, this expert will make better decisions than the average investor and therefore achieve a much better earnings rate over the long term. Thus, the investor is willing to hand over the investing of his or her funds to the expert and will pay the expert an annual fee for the advice and all other expenses associated with buying and selling securities.

Almost all investment funds are open-ended, which in effect means there is virtually no limit on the number of units that can be sold. You purchase units or shares in the fund at a price that very accurately reflects the market value of the fund's investments at any particular time. The value of a unit is simply the total value of the fund's investments after allowing for various expenses, divided by the number of units outstanding. This is also the price at which you can buy and sell units. In effect, you buy a portion of these investments when you buy units of the fund. In general, then, when the value of the fund's investments goes up, so does the value of the units. And when the value of the fund's investments goes down, so does the value of your units. The value of these units is reported in the financial pages of larger daily newspapers and in the *Financial Post* and weekly in the *Financial Times*.

The fund earns investment income throughout the year — interest, dividends, and/or capital gains. It also has expenses, including day-to-day operating expenses, commissions paid on the purchase and sale of securities, and fees for the professional management of the investments. Any profit after expenses belongs to the unit holders. With most funds, you have a choice of receiving this profit directly or having it reinvested in units of the fund. Since the investment fund units are held in your RRSP or RRIF, all interest, dividends, and capital gains are reinvested in units or shares of the fund, at no cost to you. If you redeem (sell) your units in a fund, a gain or loss results, depending on whether you redeem the units for more or less than your purchase price. The gain or loss only affects the total value of your RRSP or RRIF: there are no tax consequences.

Where to Buy Them

Units in an investment fund can be purchased through your broker and often directly from the fund itself. They can also be purchased through other financial institutions and through independent financial advisors. Investment funds must be sold *by prospectus*, which simply means that a copy of the prospectus of the fund must be supplied to you before you make your initial purchase. The prospectus outlines the investment objectives of the fund, the people involved, and certain details such as how often the units are valued for purposes of purchase and sale and what fees if any are charged if you transfer from one fund to another in a group of funds. Most funds require an initial minimum purchase, and subsequent purchases of the particular fund generally must be made in a minimum amount, usually much smaller than the initial purchase.

You might want to consider buying your funds through a mutual fund specialist, who is probably also a financial planning counsellor. However, this may not be an easy task if you have a self-directed RRSP and do not have access to such a specialist through the RRSP administrator. Bear in mind that these specialists, and most administrators of self-directed RRSPs, are usually remunerated by commissions, or front-end loads, generated from the sales of mutual funds.

The liquidity of an investment in a mutual fund depends on the particular fund. With most, you can cash your units in the fund fairly quickly, within a few days, although some funds may require a waiting period of up to a month. *Liquidity* is simply a term that refers to how quickly you can convert an investment to cash, bearing in mind any associated costs.

All funds charge a fee for the professional management of the investments, ranging from one-half per cent to two per cent of the fair market value of the fund annually. Many funds charge a front-end load fee, which ranges as high as nine per cent of the purchase price of the units. This fee can usually be reduced by purchasing units of a fund through your broker. Discount brokers offer further reductions on the front-end loads. Instead of charging a front-end load, several funds now charge a back-end load or redemption fee that usually varies depending on how long you own your units in the fund.

The front-end load is a fee deducted directly from the purchase price of the units. This fee usually represents the commission paid to the person selling you the fund. The fee also discourages individuals from buying and selling units in a fund over the short term, since the fee is not refundable. You may be able to negotiate lower fees with sellers of funds. Generally the percentage charged declines as the dollar value of your purchase increases.

Types of Funds

There are two basic types of investment funds — fixed-income funds and equity funds. These two types are usually grouped according to whether they are eligible as RRSP and RRIF investments or not. Most income funds are eligible, while a number of equity funds are not. Generally, to be eligible, a fund cannot have more than 10 per cent of its assets invested in foreign (that is, non-Canadian) securities.

Fixed-income funds invest primarily in a variety of interest-bearing investments. The earnings on your units cannot be predetermined, however, since the value of your units in the fund varies with movements in interest rates. It is the investments made by the fund that pay a fixed income, such as bonds that pay a specific rate of interest. Income funds can be broken down into several types, including bond funds, money market funds, and mortgage funds.

Equity funds invest primarily in the shares of public corporations, both Canadian and foreign, and therefore the value of these funds will increase and decrease according to the fair market value of all the fund's assets at the time of valuation. Some equity funds invest primarily in high-quality blue chip shares in order to generate dividends and respectable capital gains. Others invest in more speculative stocks and look for capital gains primarily and dividends only secondarily, while still others invest mostly in preferred shares and earn primarily dividends and little in the way of capital gains. A number of funds specialize in specific industry sectors, while the non-RRSP-eligible funds may invest primarily in one country, such as the United States or Japan, or they may be considered international funds and invest all over the world.

Balanced funds invest in both shares of public corporations and in interest-bearing securities. The manager of the fund decides which proportion of each should be held depending on current market conditions. Most balanced funds are eligible to be held by an RRSP.

Rating the Funds for Your RRSP and Your RRIF

Almost all the investment funds offered for sale in Canada are rated monthly in both the *Financial Times* and the *Financial Post*. Performance is compared over the past 10-, five-, three-

and one-year periods as well as over the previous six-, three- and one-month periods. The tables are quite detailed and provide most of the information you need to narrow down your choice of funds to only a few. Then you must make your own decisions or rely on your broker's advice as to which specific funds to buy.

When examining the ratings tables, you should first note how the funds are grouped. Primarily, they are separated into equity, income, and balanced funds, and further subdivided into those that are, or are not, eligible for your RRSP or RRIF. Money market funds, dividend funds, certain specialty funds, and even the newer funds may be separated. As well, the funds are compared as to *variability*, or the amount by which the net asset value per unit of each fund fluctuates over time. The value of aggressive funds fluctuates more widely than the value of long-term growth funds or balanced funds. Bond funds have more variability than mortgage or money market funds. The tables provide other essential pieces of information such as the size of the fund (that is, the amount invested in it), the maximum front-end load if there is one, and the manager of the fund and how long management has been with that fund. The returns over the various periods are usually expressed as net returns after all expenses, including the management fee.

You can spend days, even weeks, going over the funds — there are now well over 350 to choose from — trying to choose the best ones. Many theories abound on how to choose a good fund. But in all cases it boils down to trying to estimate future performance. Only two factors have any significant bearing on expected performance — what has the fund done in the past over the long term, and is the manager or managing group who produced those results still with the fund and expected to continue that level of performance (money market funds are excepted in both cases).

Once you have decided on the type of fund you are interested in — aggressive, long-term growth, etc. — the first thing you should look at in the table is the 10-year performance history. If the fund does not have one for 10 years (or at least seven or eight if you can get this figure from other sources) generally you should ignore it. The only exception is a newer fund that is managed by a seasoned professional with a long and successful track record. Then compare performance over the past five-year and three-year periods to ensure the fund is still performing well. Performance statistics over one- and two-year periods aren't a particularly reliable indication of how the fund might perform in the future. Economic cycles have historically lasted about four years. You want to see what a fund can do over at least two cycles before you commit your hard-earned cash. After all, how a fund performs in the bad times as well as the good should be part of your investment decision. When a fund has established a longer-term record, then you can consider it for future RRSP purchases.

Once you have picked several good performers, check out the fund manager. If it is an individual who has not been with the fund very long, ignore the fund, unless the individual has a great track record with another fund. Some investors actually follow fund managers as they move around. If it is a group, try to find out if the composition of the group has changed recently. Unfortunately, most funds don't like to divulge this type of information.

Next, you should consider eliminating those funds whose total assets are significantly smaller than the average of all funds you have been looking at. A fund with only several million dollars in assets often cannot be sufficiently diversified to avoid significant swings in value. As well, the person who successfully manages two or three million dollars may have much more trouble with 50 or 100 million. Most funds that have been around for 10 years or longer are relatively large. A number of funds have over half a billion dollars in total assets.

Finally you should consider the existence of a front-end load. Most of the better-performing funds over at least a 10-year period have front-end loads. But several do not. If you can keep the front-end load down to about five per cent, the fund need outperform a no-load fund by only about a quarter of a percentage point annually over a 20-year period to make up for the payment of the commission. Besides, many administrators of self-directed RRSPs and RRIFs may be reluctant to purchase no-load funds on your behalf. However, until you open a self-directed plan, there is no point in buying a fund with a front-end load if there is another no-load fund that you think will perform equally well. Bear in mind that your goal is to develop the best-performing RRSP or RRIF you can; it is not to avoid paying front-end loads to a broker who may be providing you with extremely valuable advice.

Since you are comparing the net appreciation in value of the various funds, that is, after allowing for all expenses, the size of

the management fee is usually not a concern since it is allowed
for when comparing performances.

Money market funds are a slightly different story. Only a few
have been around for 10 years and there is not that much difference in performance among the funds. Convenience may be a
more important factor when deciding which money market fund
to invest in. Under no circumstances should you pay a front-end
load. As well, pick one of the larger funds. Since performance
does not vary a lot from fund to fund, you should pick a fund
with a relatively low management fee.

As well, there are only a few balanced funds that have been
around for more than five years. You may have to rely on the advice of your broker to choose a good one.

Setting specific criteria for purchasing the funds will make your
investment decision much easier. The criteria outlined above eliminate up to 80 or 90 per cent of the funds very quickly, and substan-
dard performance histories should eliminate quite a few more, leaving you with a manageable handful from which to choose.

You can write to the Investment Funds Institute (see Chapter
4) for the addresses of member funds. Listed below are four of
the larger non-member funds or groups with longer-term track
records.

> Phillips Hager and North (PH&N) Group of Funds
> 1055 West Hastings Street, Suite 1700
> Vancouver, B.C. V6E 2H3
>
> Industrial Group of Funds
> Mackenzie Financial Corporation
> 150 Bloor Street West
> Toronto, Ontario M5S 2X9
>
> United Group of Funds
> United Financial Management
> 200 King Street West, Suite 1202
> Toronto, Ontario M5H 3W8
>
> Universal Group of Funds
> 401 Bay Street, Suite 1218
> Box 126, Toronto, Ontario M5H 2Y4

Many insurance companies also sell investment funds, some of which are rated in the *Financial Post* and *Financial Times*. These funds generally involve sales commissions of some variety, although most are not structured strictly as a front-end load expressed as a percentage. You are advised to carefully scrutinize these funds to ensure you are not paying commissions that are much too high for your liking.

When Should You Buy a Fund?

Of course, you would prefer to buy when prices are low and poised to go up. In real life, this doesn't happen very often. Throughout the book, it has been suggested that you use the dollar averaging method to buy shares in a fund. Establish a regular purchasing schedule and stick to it. As well, you should listen to your broker who may recommend that you weight your purchases differently depending on current market conditions. Approaches to buying funds are discussed in Chapter 4.

When Should You Sell a Fund?

This is actually a much more difficult decision to make than deciding which funds to buy. First, it cannot be stressed too often that the market goes down as well as up. Invariably, your mutual fund investments will decline in value every so often, perhaps by as much as 10 or 15 or even 20 per cent in an exceptionally bad year, simply because the market has declined. *This is not the time to sell.* All equity funds, not just your's, have probably declined in value. Just remember that, historically, the march of the stock market has been upward over the *long term*. There is no reason why history will not repeat itself.

Second, you should listen to the advice of your broker, assuming that you have your funds invested in a self-directed RRSP or RRIF. He or she will probably be aware of factors that are affecting the performance of the larger funds and maybe even your own particular funds. Third, you should probably set some ground rules and follow them no matter what, much the same as you set ground rules when you decided to dollar average your purchases. If the ground rules are reasonable (discuss them with your broker), you then avoid making investment decisions that really should be left up to the experts.

Of course, you should never run out and sell your funds just because the stock market has been declining for a week or two or interest rates are on the rise. These are *long-term* investments to be held for decades if possible. But not every choice you make will work out. A fund with a good 10-year record may lose its manager a few weeks after you buy and start sliding.

Management may make a series of horrible decisions that promise to drag down the value of the fund for years to come. Remember that not all managers are perfect. They just make better decisions most of the time than amateurs.

You should check out the performance of your funds at least once and preferably two or three times a year — and record the results or save the pieces of newspaper. Now is the time that you closely scrutinize the six-month and one- and three-year results of your fund (and two-year results also if you are keeping records). You may want to set a hard-and-fast rule that if your fund underperforms the average of all similar funds for the previous three years, it is time to sell. Or you may want to be more ruthless and use a two-year time frame.

Bear in mind, however, that all funds have a bad year now and then, for a variety of reasons. The fund manager may just have had an off-year, but he or she may also have anticipated a major sector movement a year too early. If you sell at the end of that year, you could miss out on some big gains.

The existence of relatively hefty front-end loads and redemption fees should discourage you from switching funds too often and, hopefully, encourage you to do your homework before you buy.

The worst thing you can do is compare your funds with others on a monthly basis. You will almost always find one and maybe a dozen that are performing better than yours each and every month. But you will find far fewer that outperform yours on a two- or three-year basis. And definitely remember to compare funds that are similar, that is, funds that have similar variabilities and that are of the same type and either are or are not RRSP- and RRIF-eligible.

Canada Savings Bonds (CSBs)

Most Canadians have bought, or have considered buying, CSBs at some point, often through a payroll savings plan at their place of employment. CSBs are also available from financial institutions and brokers in denominations of $100 and larger. You will buy your CSBs from the administrator of your self-directed RRSP or RRIF. They only go on sale toward the end of October of each year, and sales are cut off about the first of November. An upper annual purchase limit is usually imposed ($75,000 recently), although there is no limit to the number of new CSBs that you can acquire with cash from old CSBs which mature in that year.

The interest on CSBs is paid annually on November 1 by direct deposit to your self-directed RRSP or RRIF. There are also compound interest CSBs that pay interest on maturity, usually seven to 10 years from the date of purchase. These are much more suitable for your RRSP or RRIF since you do not have to worry about reinvesting the annual interest payments.

Keep in mind that the interest rate at which new CSBs are advertised is guaranteed for only one year. After that, the interest on the bond is set each year according to current interest rates, although a minimum rate is guaranteed to be paid to maturity.

CSBs are different from all other bonds, in that they can be cashed in at any time for their face value. You also receive any interest earned up to the end of the preceding month. Thus, if you plan to cash in a CSB, wait until the beginning of a month so you receive the extra interest. If the CSB is cashed before February in the year following the date of purchase (three months), no interest is payable.

Canada Savings Bonds are one of the best and easiest short- to medium-term interest-bearing investments you can make. With a CSB, you will participate in any interest rate increases as the government raises the rate payable on the bond periodically to match other rates, but you are protected from significant interest rate declines since a minimum rate is guaranteed to be paid on the bond.

Pension Reform

T HE PENSION REFORM proposals that have been introduced over the last few years are scheduled for implementation in 1987 through to 1995. It appears that all pension plans will be affected, since the provinces have agreed in principle to institute pension standards reforms almost identical to those implemented by the federal government. Only the question of indexing pension benefits to increases in the cost of living remains unresolved. The pension reform proposals should make pensions more accessible to more Canadians, and many more Canadians should be able to provide adequately for their retirement years without undue dependence on the Government.

Nevertheless, no matter how good you might think your pension plan is, you should always attempt to contribute as much as possible to your RRSP each and every year. There is no guarantee that your plan will always be as good as it is now, or that you will always be working for that employer, or that your employer will even exist in a few years time. However, your RRSP will always be there whether you change jobs, or your job and company disappear. As well, considering the flexibility of RRSPs, there is no point in not contributing if you are otherwise planning to invest extra cash.

The pension reform proposals focus on three primary areas: putting all pension plans on the same footing regarding tax assistance for contributions and consequently benefits, making pension plans more accessible to more workers, and improving benefits for a large number of workers. There are three major types of pension plans: employer-sponsored defined benefit plans, employer-sponsored money purchase or defined contribution plans, and self-contributory RRSPs — also considered to be money purchase plans, which were originally designed to act as a pension plan for the self-employed and for employees who do not have access to a company-sponsored plan. Deferred profit sharing plans (DPSPs) also benefit from pension reform.

Under a defined benefit RPP (registered pension plan), a certain pension is guaranteed to be paid. The employer, with or without the financial help of the employee, provides the necessary funding to pay the required pension. Over 90 per cent of employees who are covered by pension plans are members of defined benefit plans. Under money purchase plans, the employee and the employer contribute to the plan, and the best pension possible is purchased with the accumulated funds in the plan when the employee retires.

Non-Contributory Reforms

The major non-contributory, or pension standards, reforms affecting employer-sponsored RPPs generally took effect by January 1, 1987 federally and in a number of provinces, and include:

Eligibility for Membership.   Full-time workers will be eligible to join a plan after two years of service with the employer, and part-time workers will be able to join after they have earned at least 35 per cent of the average industrial wage in each of two consecutive years.

Vesting (the time at which the employee attains the right to pension benefits resulting from both his or her and the employer's contributions). Vesting will occur after the employee has been a member of the plan for two years no matter what the employee's age, instead of the standard 10 years and age 45.

Refunding.   On termination of employment, the employee's contributions that have not vested must be returned, plus a reasonable rate of interest.

Employer's Contributions.   The employer must pay for at least half the value of any pension earned under a defined benefit plan, which generally means the employer must, at a minimum, contribute as much to the plan as the employee. Alternatively, in some jurisdictions the employer may have the option of providing indexed benefits under the plan.

Portability. When changing employers, employees will generally be able to choose from several options: (a) leave their vested pension benefits on account with their former employer and eventually receive a pension; (b) receive an early pension if they are within 10 years of the normal retirement date specified in the pension plan; (c) transfer their pension entitlement to their new employer; or (d) transfer their benefits to a locked-in RRSP (a variation on normal RRSPs, where the employee will not have access to the RRSP funds except to receive a retirement income).

Early Retirement. Pension plans will allow for early retirement 10 years prior to the normal retirement age stated in the plan.

Survivor Benefits. A plan must provide for benefits to continue to be paid to a surviving spouse at a minimum of 60 per cent of the full benefit rate, even if the spouse remarries; a surviving spouse is also entitled to the full accrued benefits of a plan member who dies before retirement.

Women's Pensions. Every pension plan must guarantee to pay the same benefits to men and women retiring under the same circumstances.

Marriage Breakdown. All plans must permit the splitting of pension benefit entitlements between spouses on the breakdown of the marriage.

Information Disclosure. Plans must provide information about earned benefits and accumulated contributions to members and their spouses every year. As well, a majority of plan members may require representation by members and pensioners on pension management committees.

Inflation Protection. Only Ontario and Nova Scotia are committed to including some type of inflation protection in their provincial pension standards legislation. What form this inflation protection will take has not been revealed.

Contributory Reforms

The intent of the pension reform is to put RRSPs and other money purchase RPPs on the same footing as defined benefit RPPs, at least as far as contributing and providing pension benefits. In the past, defined benefit RPPs have been able to provide much larger maximum pension benefits than money purchase plans. The contributory reforms for RRSPs and RPPs in connection with RRSP contributions were outlined in Chapter 3. Additional information is provided below on the mechanism for determining the pension adjustment (PA) for purposes of making an RRSP contribution by members of defined benefit registered pension plans. If you know the details of your pension plan, you may be able to get a rough approximation of your RRSP contribution room.

Your RRSP contribution room is reduced by an amount that reflects the value of contribution room taken up by the RPP in the previous year. The PA in this case is calculated generally as:

(9 x Benefit Entitlement) minus $600

The *nine times factor* recognizes that, on average, it takes approximately nine dollars to fund every one dollar of pension income annually on retirement. The $600 is an *ad hoc* figure established in recognition of the fact that not all pension plans provide the same benefits. The benefit entitlement represents the pension benefit accrued during the previous year. It is based on the structure of the particular plan. For example, if a plan has a single benefit rate of 1.5 per cent of the best average three consecutive years for each year of service, and the employee's pensionable earnings over the whole of 1990 (generally salary or wages) are $38,000, the benefit entitlement will be calculated as follows:

Benefit entitlement = .015 (1.5 per cent) x $38,000 = $570.

The PA would then be calculated as:

PA = (9 x $570) - $600 = $4,530.

The employee's RRSP contribution room in 1991 would be the lesser of $8,500 and 18 per cent of $38,000 minus PA of $4,530 = $6,840 minus $4,530 = $2,310.

If the employee were entitled to a maximum pension of two per cent of pensionable earnings, his or her maximum allowable RRSP contribution would be only $600. Bear in mind that not all defined benefit RPPs are the same, so adjustments to the PA calculation will be made. For example, if the benefit rate in the plan is 1.5 per cent of *average career earnings*, not best three years, the benefit entitlement will be reduced accordingly since a smaller pension will eventually be paid, and you will be able to contribute more to your RRSP.

Two other adjustments can be made to total contribution room available in any given year. Benefits in respect of prior years that occur after 1988 (past service credits) under your company-sponsored pension plan can generally be increased only to the extent of total RRSP contribution room available. If past service RPP benefits are increased, RRSP contribution room is adjusted downward correspondingly (called the past service pension adjustment PSPA). Occasionally, RPP benefits may be reduced or eliminated; for example, you may leave your job and receive a refund of RPP contributions because your benefits have not vested. In this situation, total RRSP contribution room can be restored under the pension adjustment reversal (PAR) mechanism.

Special Situations

Marriage Breakdown

Divorce law (family law) in most provinces now requires that family assets accumulated during the marriage be split evenly on divorce or breakdown of the marriage. This law generally extends to unmarried couples who have been living together for a time and have children. Amounts in RRSPs and RRIFs would generally constitute family assets. These amounts usually must be divided up into pre-marriage and during-marriage portions.

When a marriage breaks down, amounts in one spouse's RRSP or RRIF can be transferred to the RRSP or RRIF of the other spouse with no tax consequences. This is not possible while you are still married and living together. Amounts can also be transferred to the other spouse's company pension plan. To qualify for the tax-free transfer, the payments from one plan to another must be made according to a decree, order, or judgement of a competent tribunal (usually a court) or a written separation agreement arising as a result of the breakdown of the marriage. The spousal RRSP rules that require amounts to be included in the income of the contributing spouse if the RRSP is cancelled within three years of the contribution are not invoked in the case of marriage breakdown.

You cannot make such transfers just to put more funds in one spouse's hands so that he or she will have more income during retirement. You must avail yourself of spousal RRSPs.

If you are receiving annuity payments from an RRSP and are ordered to transfer them to an estranged spouse, you must include the amounts in your income for tax purposes, and then deduct the amount paid to the estranged spouse. The payment would be a normal alimony or maintenance payment and hence be taxable in the recipient spouse's hands.

If you are ordered to make a lump-sum payment and you are retired and receiving an RRSP annuity, you might be able to arrange for a portion of the annuity to be commuted. You would first transfer the commuted amount into an RRIF and then transfer the amount to the estranged spouse's RRIF. Structuring the payment this way avoids the payment of any tax and should permit both spouses to receive or keep more than they otherwise could have.

What Happens to Your RRSP or RRIF if You Take Up Residence in Another Country?

This question can be extremely complex and almost everybody should seek professional advice, primarily to avoid paying too much tax which could be substantial if you have large amounts in your RRSP or RRIF.

In most cases, you will not get to take all of the funds in your RRSP or RRIF with you. Canada has given you tax deductions for your contributions and it would like to see some of its tax dollars come back if you leave the country with your RRSP. If you leave it here intact, you may escape Canadian tax for the time being, but you will pay it eventually. However, your new country may not recognize your RRSP as a tax shelter (which it is) and tax the income earned in the RRSP. If you withdraw funds from the RRSP, Canada will generally levy a withholding tax and your new country of residence might also tax the payments, or at least the income earned in the RRSP since you left Canada, but you will probably get credit for any Canadian tax paid. On the other hand, Canada may exempt RRIF or RRSP annuity payments from tax if you are a resident of a country with which Canada has an appropriate tax treaty. As a non-resident, you can even file a Canadian tax return and receive relatively small amounts from your RRSP free of Canadian tax. However, your new country of residence will probably tax the amounts.

The permutations and combinations are virtually endless, making it impossible to generalize in any meaningful way. But a tax professional (lawyer or chartered accountant) can straighten things out for you. *Don't attempt to do it by yourself*, even if you are only a little bit baffled by the Canadian tax system. The fee you pay to the professional, and it may be substantial, will be well worth it. There are a variety of ways to reduce your tax bill and put more RRSP or RRIF money in your pocket, all of which are perfectly legal.

In the year that you leave Canada, you can contribute to your RRSP, if there is any advantage in doing so, to a maximum based on your Canadian earned income of that year and any contribution room available from prior years.

What Happens to Your RRSP Should You Die?

Very simply, amounts in your RRSP go to your heirs, that is the person or persons you specify in your will or in your RRSP or RRIF contract. The real question is how much cash will be left when your heirs finally receive the RRSP or RRIF amounts after all taxes are paid?

First, you should ensure that you have named specific beneficiaries of your RRSP or RRIF in your Will or RRSP contract. Generally, the provisions of your Will should override any provisions in the RRSP contract, if you drafted your Will after signing the RRSP contract. The executors of your estate will have an easier time if you are careful to name specific beneficiaries. As explained below, there are tax reasons for naming specific people to get RRSP amounts while other heirs would receive some of your other assets.

Generally, your spouse will be able to receive all RRSP and RRIF amounts free of tax, assuming that he or she meets certain conditions.

If your RRSP *has not matured* (that is, you have not yet arranged to receive a retirement income), essentially, your spouse (which includes a common-law spouse), if he or she is named as beneficiary, steps into your shoes and becomes the owner of the plan if your spouse is age 71 or less. There are no tax consequences to this transfer of ownership. If your spouse was not specifically named as a beneficiary, or is over age 71, the executor of your estate can elect for your spouse to receive a *refund of premiums* from the RRSP, which simply means that he or she receives all amounts in the RRSP. Your spouse then can transfer this refund of premiums within 60 days after the year end to his or her own RRSP or RRIF with no tax consequences. The spouse may also buy an RRSP annuity with the refund of premiums. Any amount not transferred must be included in the spouse's income for tax purposes in the year it is received.

Refund of premium amounts can also be paid to your dependent children or grandchildren, *if you do not have a spouse at the time of your death*. A child is dependent if the child's income was not in excess of $5,000 in the year before you die and the child is not claimed as a dependent by someone else on a tax return. The amount that each child can receive as a refund of premiums is $5,000 multiplied by the number resulting when the age of the child is subtracted from 26. However, the child must include this amount in income for tax purposes. It cannot be transferred to the child's RRSP.

Children who are physically and mentally infirm may receive a refund of premiums in any amount. Like a spouse, they have the option of transferring the amount to an RRSP or RRIF or buying an RRSP annuity within 60 days after the year end.

If RRSP amounts do not go to your spouse or children, they are taxed in your final income tax return. If large amounts have accumulated, the RRSP could be taxed at rates as high as 50 per cent depending on your province of residence. Thus, all this tax may be deferred if the RRSP goes to your spouse. If refund of premium amounts go to your children, they will probably pay much less tax than will be payable in your final tax return. There is no point in paying the Government more than they expect, so why not take the few minutes to think about RRSP beneficiaries and then word your Will accordingly.

If your RRSP *has matured*, that is, you are now receiving a retirement income, the rules are quite similar if you have everything in an RRIF. The spouse can take over ownership of the RRIF and receive all payments, or the spouse can receive a refund of premiums. If there is no spouse, children can receive a refund of premiums.

If your RRSP has matured and you were receiving an RRSP annuity at the time of your death, different rules apply. With a joint and last survivor annuity, your spouse simply continues to receive the payments. With fixed-term annuities and life annuities that still have a guaranteed payment period remaining, the spouse may become the annuitant, in which case the spouse receives all future payments and no tax is payable on your RRSP in your final tax return. The executor of your estate can elect for your spouse to become the annuitant or receive a refund of premiums in respect of the annuity (a lump-sum payment from the annuity issuer would have to be arranged). Amounts received by your spouse from an RRSP annuity or an RRIF as a consequence of your death are eligible for the pension income tax credit, even though your spouse has not reached age 65.

Glossary of Terms

Accrued Income.   Income earned and credited to you, but not considered to be received for tax purposes. Also called *deferred income*. Interest may accrue on GICs or capital gains may accrue on equity fund investments.

Amortization.   Generally, the period of time over which a debt is allocated or spread out. Mortgages may be amortized over 25 years, which means if you stick to the repayment schedule you will pay off your mortgage in exactly 25 years.

Annuitant.   The person who receives payments from an annuity; also the person who will eventually receive retirement income from an RRSP.

Annuity.   A financial instrument, usually purchased with a large sum, that provides periodic payment of principal and interest over a particular length of time.

Arm's-Length.   Describes a transaction where there is no special relationship among interested parties that would cause them to ignore fair market value.

Assessment Notice.   Official notification of your tax liability from Revenue Canada.

Attribution Rules.   Tax legislation that, in certain instances, makes you taxable on income earned on assets which you have transferred to your spouse or to a child under 18 years of age.

Balanced Fund. A mutual fund that invests in both interest-bearing securities and shares of public corporations.

Bear Market. A general decline in the value of publicly traded shares on the stock market.

Beneficiary. Person entitled to the funds from an insurance policy when the insured person dies; also the person entitled to benefit from a trust or other financial arrangement.

Blue Chip Stocks. The shares of large, well-established corporations with a history of good earnings and dividend payments.

Bull Market. A general increase in the value of publicly traded shares on the stock market.

Bond Fund. A mutual fund that invests primarily in short-, medium-, and long-term government and corporate bonds.

Canada Deposit Insurance. Insurance carried by banks and most trust companies protecting individual depositors against losses up to a total of $60,000.

Capital Gain or Loss. The difference between the sale price of a capital property and the purchase price after allowing for all costs of purchase and sale.

Capital Property. Securities or physical property, such as real estate, that may increase or decrease in value and on which a gain or loss may be realized on disposition.

Cash Surrender Value. The value of a permanent or whole life insurance policy if it is cancelled. Term policies have no value except on the death of the insured.

Collateral. Property pledged as security for a loan. A mortgage is simply a loan with your home as collateral. If you default on the loan, the mortgagee (the bank) can sell your home to recover the amount of the loan.

Consumer Price Index (CPI). Measures month-to-month changes in the cost of living or inflation.

Common Shares. Shares that represent a portion of ownership in a corporation allowing the owners of those shares to participate in the increase or decrease in the fortunes of the company. May have voting rights and dividends may be paid on the shares.

Deferred Income. Income already earned but not yet reported for tax purposes.

Defined Benefit Pension Plan. A pension plan under which a specific pension is guaranteed to be paid. The employer, often with the help of the employee, then supplies sufficient funding to provide those benefits.

Dividend Tax Credit. Reduces the amount of personal tax paid on dividends from Canadian corporations; intended to compensate for tax already paid by the corporation paying the dividend.

Dollar Cost Averaging. The purchase of a specific investment, such as units or shares in a mutual fund, at specific intervals, such as monthly.

Equity. Ownership interest in a property. Can be represented by shares in a corporation, the value of which reflect the changing worth of the company.

Face Amount. Amount stated on a life insurance policy to be paid if the insured should die.

Fair Market Value. The amount that a willing buyer would pay and a willing seller would accept in an open and unrestricted market, assuming that both parties are knowledgeable, are dealing at arm's length, and neither is under any compulsion to act.

Fixed Income. Rate of return stated on an investment to be earned over a particular period of time; not applicable to income investment funds that may invest in fixed-income investments.

Front-End Load. A sales charge, or commission, applied on the purchase of units in an investment fund; deducted from the amount invested.

Indexing. Periodic increases in a series of payments, often tied to a specific percentage or to increases in the Consumer Price Index.

International Fund. A mutual fund that invests in shares and/or interest-bearing securities around the world, not primarily in Canadian securities.

Joint and Last Survivor Annuity. An annuity under which payments continue to either person named as an annuitant, even after the death of one of the persons named.

Leverage. Using borrowed money to increase the amount invested and, hopefully, the rate of return on the investment.

Liquidity. A measure of how readily an investment can be converted to cash without incurring a penalty or a loss in the value of the investment.

Margin. Situation where you borrow from your broker for the purchase of securities which are, in effect, lodged as collateral against the loan. The term *margin* refers to the amount of cash put up by the investor for the purchase. RRSPs cannot be margined.

Marginal Rate of Tax. Tax rate applied to the last dollar of income earned in the year, which is the portion of income that is taxed most heavily.

Money Market. Part of the capital market devoted to short-term lending and borrowing of money.

Money Market Fund. A mutual fund that invests exclusively in money market securities.

Money Purchase Pension Plan. A pension plan under which the employer and employee contribute specific amounts and the best pension possible is purchased with the accumulated funds (also called a *defined contribution plan*).

Net Income. For tax purposes, the amount determined after deducting RRSP and pension plan contributions, union and professional dues, child care, and various other expenses.

Net RRSP Investment. The amount contributed to your RRSP after allowing for your tax reduction. This is the same after-tax amount that could be invested outside an RRSP.

Opportunity Cost. Also called *alternative investment cost*. The amount you could have earned if you had chosen to invest your funds elsewhere.

Portfolio. All the securities owned by an individual, whether inside or outside an RRSP.

Preferred Shares. Issued by a corporation after the distribution of common shares. Preferred shares carry dividends at specific rates, which must be paid before dividends are paid on common shares.

Present Value. The value of something in the future expressed in terms of its value today. Present value is used to ensure that dollars in the future are measured and therefore compared accurately. A dollar in 1992 and 1998 will not have the same purchasing power. If both are expressed in terms of their value today, they can be compared meaningfully.

Prime Lending Rate. The lowest interest rate at which banks lend money, usually to their best customers. The rate at which you can borrow may be expressed as prime plus a specific per cent. Only the best credit risks (usually large corporations) can borrow at prime, unless you offer first-rate security for the loan, such as a mortgage on your home.

Principal Residence. The tax term for the home that you own and in which you live. Any gain realized on the sale of your home is tax-exempt. Families are allowed this exemption on only one owner-occupied home after 1981, but for gains arising before 1982, each spouse may claim an exemption on one owner-occupied home, which could include a vacation property.

Prospectus. A legal document describing securities being offered for sale to the public. Investment funds must generally be sold by prospectus, which simply means that you must be furnished with a copy of the prospectus of the particular fund before you can buy units or shares in the fund for the first time.

Superannuation. Very much the same as a pension.

Tax Credits. Amounts subtracted from tax payable (usually federal tax), such as the child tax credit or political contribution tax credit. Most tax credits subtracted from federal tax act to reduce provincial tax payable.

Tax Instalments. Tax payments that must be made every three months to Revenue Canada by individuals who are self-employed or have a substantial amount of investment or other income on which tax is not withheld by the payer of the income.

Taxable Income. The amount left on your tax return after taking all eligible deductions or exemptions. Tax is calculated on this figure. For many taxpayers, net income and taxable income will be similar.

Trust. Very simply, the holding of property (usually investments) by one person (the trustee) for the benefit of another person (the beneficiary). A *settlor* transfers the property to the trustee (often the same person). A properly established trust is considered a separate entity for tax purposes.

Index